What People Are Saying About
Choose to Be Happy...

"Most people wonder how they can lead a happier life. Rima Rudner has learned by experience how to turn life's lemons into positive opportunities. Her easy to read, practical views get right to the heart of the common causes of unhappiness. Each chapter offers practical "how to" to help readers cope when life isn't all they hoped it would be."

Alison Blackman Dunham
Life and Career Expert
Creator of Advice Sisters Online Publications

"Rima Rudner is my hero! I have developed motivation programs for years in health care. In these endeavors, I have been a junkie for "how to" material. This book is simply the finest self-help book I have ever read. I keep thinking of more and more loved ones that I need to supply a copy. Rima attacks the issues of happiness from every perceivable angle and provides magnificently simple strategies and solutions. Brilliant content, carefully presented, I LOVE this book."

Michael J. O'Malley
Motivational Speaker

"Rima Rudner is a genius! She has crystallized the essence of what all the experts have been saying about happiness and fused the information with her humor and stories. This book is a delight to read as well as food for the heart and soul. A great choice for anyone who wants to explore all angles of the very important business of happiness!"

Lisa Kamen
"Happiness Promoter"
www.whatisyourhappiness.com

"Rima gives the reader new insights that can lead to inner peace. I will live by her 'Fifteen Percent Principle' for the rest of my life. Add the 'Wait 24 Hours Rule' and you have a winning combination! In addition, Rudner provides a list of razor sharp 'Happiness Rules' in the final pages of the book to be used as a happiness factor jumpstart every morning. She immediately welcomes you into her life and makes you feel at home. It's moving, it's frank, and it's alive with her voice of encouragement."

Nicole Merritt
MyShelf.com

"This is a wonderful new self-help book that expands on the concept of 'The Secret' – that positive thoughts bring positive results. The author gives her readers new insights and practical 'Happiness Tools' that make this book a must read for anyone who wants to improve the quality of their lives. Ms. Rudner proves that happiness is at least 50% genetic and that anyone can overcome their genetic unhappiness by refusing to be a victim. She teaches you how to reprogram your inner thoughts, create abundance, develop your intuition, get rid of toxic people, and stop worrying forever. I LOVED IT!"

Kathy Jameson
TheBooxReview.com

"This book is loaded! Tens of thousands of dollars and years of psychotherapy boiled down into one book. Like a shotgun loaded with solutions for happiness, this book is ULTRA-comprehensive, wise and real. It deserves a spot on the quick reference book shelf for guidance to happiness in any solution. For anyone who wants more happiness and is ready to take action, pull the trigger with Rudner."

Steve Sorkin
"A-HA Performance"
Co-creator and Contributing Author

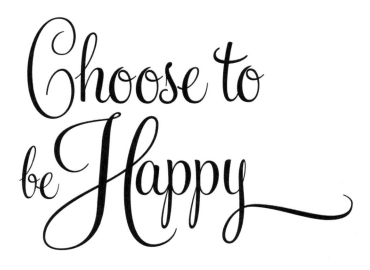

Choose to be Happy

A GUIDE TO TOTAL HAPPINESS

Rima Rudner

❤ Choose, Inc. Publishing

♥ Choose, Inc. Publishing LLC

www.choosetobehappy.net
Email: rima@rimarudner.com

Distributed by Atlas Books

www.AtlasBooks.com
800-247-6553 or 800-266-5564

Library of Congress Control Number: 2008923489

ISBN-10: 0-9801096-0-4

ISBN-13: 978-0-9801096-0-3

10 9 8 7 6 5 4 3 2

With love, I dedicate this book to my husband, Harvey,
our children, Lara and Stacey,
and to all my dear friends who have become part of my family
and have stood by me through thick and thin.
You have all made my life worth living
and this book worth writing.
I love you all!

The Constitution only gives people the right to pursue happiness. You have to catch it yourself.

—Ben Franklin

If you want others to be happy, practice compassion. If you want to be happy, practice compassion.

—The Dalai Lama

Happiness depends upon ourselves.

—Aristotle

Think of all the beauty that is still left in and around you and be happy!

—Anne Frank

Happiness comes from spiritual wealth, not material wealth... Happiness comes from giving, not getting. If we try hard to bring happiness to others, we cannot stop it from coming to us also. To get joy, we must give it, and to keep joy, we must scatter it.

—John Templeton

Table of Contents

Foreword

My colleague, Auke Tellegen, and I published in 1996 a report of our study of the happiness scores of a very large sample of middle-aged twins. One's psychological well-being varies of course from time to time, due to the slings and arrows, but it returns—in hours, days, or a few months at most—to a kind of set-point that is characteristic of one's self. Tellegen and I had found that the level of this happiness set point is strongly determined by genetic factors. For that reason, we suggested that trying to be happier may be like trying to be taller. I regretted that statement as soon as I saw it in print and I got to work writing a book that would set the record straight. My book, *Happiness*, Golden Books, was in press when Rima Rudner sent me the manuscript of her *Choose to Be Happy* and I was delighted by the way in which the two books fit together. Mine focuses on the research that tells us what we know about happiness, why most people are happy most of the time, and why certain behaviors raise us up above our innate set points while other ways of acting drag us down again, the tendencies I call "happiness thieves." *Choose to Be Happy*, on the other hand, is a rich compendium of sensible, creative ideas and maxims for combating those "happiness thieves," a handbook for those who, because of bad habits or unfortunate inheritance, are being cheated of the sense of personal well-being to which all of us aspire.

Rima Rudner is not a scientist or a therapist. She is instead a very smart, perceptive woman who took herself in hand as an adult and cured herself of the misery and self-doubt that she seems to have inherited from her parents. Along the way, she must have kept a diary because her book is rich with fascinating examples. *Choose to Be Happy* is like a personal trainer for people determined to build up their muscles of self-confidence and their ability to enjoy living. Ms. Rudner knows all about the downside because she's been there and she also knows how to move to the upside, because she's done that too.

By the late *Dr. David T. Lykken*

Introduction

If you bought this book you have taken the first step to achieving happiness—admitting that you need help in attaining the level of happiness you deserve. The United States Declaration of Independence states that every person has the "right to life, liberty and the pursuit of happiness." Note that we don't have a *right* to happiness, but rather a *right to "pursue"* happiness. This means that it's up to you to find happiness—so let's get started.

First, what is happiness? In order to find something we have to define what it is that we are looking for. But happiness doesn't have the same meaning for everyone. Some people see happiness as the absence of unhappiness. Others see it as just having fun. But for most of us, the happiness we seek has a much deeper meaning.

Is the pursuit of happiness selfish? *Absolutely not!*. People don't enjoy being around people who are unhappy. If you are genuinely happy you will radiate happy energy onto those around you. In return, you will receive happy energy back. It's a win-win situation for everyone.

Life is full of obstacles. You jump over one hurdle and a new one appears. Sometimes you can overcome these obstacles, sometimes you can't. But it's your *attitude* about these hurdles that will allow you to be happy instead of sad or angry.

Happiness doesn't just happen. It requires hard work and self-discipline, as does everything in life that's worth pursuing. In order to possess true happiness, you need to develop wisdom and compassion. But even more than that, you need to find a way to see humor in *everything*.

I decided to write this book because I come from a genetically-unhappy family and have always had to work very hard to fight my underlying sadness. I work at refusing to be unhappy with the same commitment and self-control that a recovering alcoholic uses when he refuses to take a sip of wine. This includes not only retraining my inner thoughts to be positive instead of negative, but also eliminating toxic people and negative situations from my life. After many years of hard work, I have finally become the happy person I've always wanted to be despite the many tragic events that have marred my life. Now I want to share with you the wisdom I've learned in the process.

My best girlfriend, Elizabeth, is always happy. She gets out of bed singing and full of enthusiasm every morning. She is incredibly energetic and has a zest for life. If you tell her a story about somebody evil or a negative event, she will always find something positive to say about that person or event.

Over the years I've asked her repeatedly to share her "secret" of happiness. She keeps on insisting that she was born happy and that she comes from a genetically happy, fun-loving family. She has always just assumed that happiness just meant having fun and purposely refuses to sabotage her happiness by not allowing any negative input to infiltrate her mind.

Lydia is genetically happy, too. I ask her, "Is everyone in your family as happy as you are?"

She thinks for a moment, says "Yep," and proceeds to tell me that she sets her alarm for 5:00 A.M. every morning, even on weekends when she doesn't have to get up early for work.

I look at her like she's crazy. "Why?"

"Because while I'm sleeping I don't know whether I'm having fun or not, but when I'm awake I always know I'm having fun," she responds.

To believe that happiness equals fun is a simple concept, however, I am not implying either Elizabeth or Lydia is a simpleton. On the contrary, I am implying that they are both much wiser than most unhappy people who don't usually think in simple concepts. I am a genetically unhappy person and I used to make my life much more complex than it needed to be—a trait of most unhappy people.

When I was in interior design school and we were asked to create a design problem and then find a solution, I would think of the most difficult problem with the most complex solution in order to challenge myself. I would spend twice as many hours on homework as anyone else. On the day we presented our projects to the class I was amazed at how simple everyone else's project seemed. I asked myself, "Why am I making life so difficult for myself? I realized that the best solution to even the most difficult problem is the simplest solution.

❧ *Life doesn't have to be complex unless you make it complex.* ❧

In spite of this wisdom, when I tried to be like Elizabeth and Lydia and planned my life so that I was always having fun, there would always be a little voice inside me nagging, "You're not happy. There's something missing in your life." And there was—it was a *purpose*. I realized that I was just one of those people who couldn't be happy unless I was fulfilling a need to add something to world, which is the main reason why I am writing this book.

I am the poster child for overcoming genetic unhappiness. As far back as I can remember there has been one life crisis after another in my life and I was able to get through each and every crisis by finding humor in it. I realized that it is not what happens to you that makes you happy or unhappy; it is how you *perceive* what happens to you.

Lest you think I'm full of poop, let me give you a rundown of the obstacles I've triumphed over. First, when I was a young child, my mother was undergoing shock treatments for severe depression and unable to cope with being a mother. She would say demeaning things to me like "You inherited the Rudner fat legs." Or, "Your sister is the smart one. You'd better marry a professional who can take care of you." This did wonders for my self-esteem.

My sister, who was 3 ½ years older than I, hated my existence so much that she wouldn't have anything to do with me. My mother told me that when she and my father brought me home from the hospital, my sister was so jealous of me that she tore apart a feather pillow with her teeth. All I can remember about my sister is her screaming and yelling, kicking me out of her room, and throwing herself on the living room floor kicking and screaming until she got what she wanted.

My family used to go out to dinner together every Sunday night. I remember that my father refused to order that nice juicy steak he really wanted because it was fifty cents or a dollar more than he thought he should spend, although he could well afford it. When he was in his mid-forties he got cancer of the larynx. It wasn't long until he had a tracheotomy and could no longer eat foods that needed chewing. As the cancer progressed, he had to be fed through a tube. I remember well the smell of the cancer that permeated our home.

How sad that he never got to experience the taste and texture of that succulent filet mignon. I realized that we should never deny ourselves experiences that will give us pleasure because we never know what our future holds. When life offers you enjoyment, accept it graciously, as if it is a precious gift.

❧ Live each day as if it is your last! (And hope it isn't.) ❧

When my mother was around 50 years old, she was on the way to the cleaners to pick up a dress for my sister's second wedding, which was to take place that evening. My mother accidentally (I think) drove her brand new Buick Riviera over a 500-foot cliff. She was thrown from the car and landed on top of a garage. I rushed to the hospital where I was told that "if" she lived they would have to amputate one of her legs. They told me that I would have to sign for the surgery. I did, even though I was only 21 years old. I tried to contact my sister, but she had decided to go ahead with her wedding and then left on her two-week honeymoon in Mexico. For six months I was at the hospital day and night. Luckily, my mother lived, despite having every bone in her body broken. My sister got another divorce and moved to New York, leaving me to take care of my mother.

When I was about 24 years old, my then-husband and I adopted a child. We had tried to conceive our own, but one of us was apparently infertile. My sister, who had just had a miscarriage, told me that I was the cause of our fertility problems and made up some story that she saw my father treating a suspicious large birthmark on my private parts with radioactive material when I was an infant and that probably caused me to become infertile. My mother-in-law told me that it must be my fault since her son had once knocked up a girl. These two malicious people purposely tried to make me feel bad about myself. My mistake was that I *let* them hurt me.

*❧ No one can make you feel bad or hurt you unless you **let** them. ❧*

When our adopted daughter was 3 ½ we got a divorce. My ex found a girlfriend whom he eventually married. This not-very-nice woman said to me "I've always wanted a daughter of my own" and proceeded to brainwash my daughter against me. When my daughter was sent home prematurely from a teen tour because she was stealing from stores, I insisted that she had to live by the rules of my home.

She screamed obscenities at me and went to live with my ex and his wife. My daughter would no longer talk to me. I was devastated. While we were estranged, she became a drug addict, committed crimes, and was eventually arrested for the manufacture of methamphetamines and faced 7 ½ years of hard time in a state prison—a long enough story for another book.

My mother developed Alzheimer's disease when she was around 70 years old and died in a nursing home when she was about 80, having found childlike happiness only after almost every one of her brain cells had died. I took care of her alone. My sister wouldn't even come to the funeral, but she *was* available to collect her inheritance.

My aunt was an old spinster who had lived with her parents in the Bronx until they died. She moved to Los Angeles because she was tired of getting mugged in New York. (Of course, don't think she didn't get mugged her first week in Los Angeles.) She spent her entire life alone, pinching pennies and drinking free coffee at the bank as she fondled her stack of bank books that she had stashed in her safe deposit box. She died of Alzheimer's a few years before my mother. I took care of her, too.

Naturally, I believed that I was condemned to a genetic destiny of cancer, Alzheimer's disease and unhappiness. I was smoking more than two packs of cigarettes a day and was always sick. I tormented myself with thoughts about getting cancer. I visualized myself growing one of those grotesque huge brown tumors I used to see pictures of in my father's radiology books. In fact, I was already starting to show symptoms and diagnosed with first stage emphysema and Reynaud's disease in my late twenties. And still, I didn't stop smoking. I was clearly self-destructive. It's obvious to me now that there is a direct correlation between addictive behavior, which I consider a form of self-abuse, and unhappiness.

Right after my divorce, the words, "Look what you're done to me," used to play themselves over and over again in my mind like a broken record. I truly blamed my unhappiness on my ex-husband. In my mind, it was his fault I was unhappy. I was a *victim*. I realize now that unhappy people usually need someone on whom to blame their unhappiness. You cannot be a victim and be happy at the same time—it is impossible because victims are never happy and happy people are never victims. Happy people take responsibility for everything that happens to them. They know how to turn negative events into positive learning experiences.

When I was 38 year old I met Harvey, the man I married. A few years after we met, we were up at Lake Tahoe skiing and I caught a flu, which turned into pleurisy and then escalated into pneumonia. I had a hacking cough, but I was still chain smoking. When the doctor told me there was no chance I would get better if I didn't stop smoking, I finally realized that I was the same age as my father was when he first got cancer of the larynx. I had a vivid memory of my helpless morphine-filled father lying in his hospital bed with a tracheotomy tube stuck in his neck and a nurse suctioning out the mucous. That was the day that I realized that the small amount of self-control and discomfort I would have to endure temporarily was far less than the pain and suffering that I would have to endure if I continued my self-destructive behavior. That day I decided to defy my genetic unhappiness with the same resolution that an Olympic athlete uses when he or she trains for the Olympics.

I realized that I could never be happy if I felt helpless and that a prerequisite to happiness was to be in control over my life. Cigarettes were not only affecting the quality of my life, but also had actually taken away the control I had over my life.

I decided that I wanted to look and feel better physically in order to enjoy the quality of life that I somehow now miraculously believed I deserved. Step one to achieving happiness was to stop smoking.

I had previously spent many thousands of dollars on four or five different stop-smoking programs. I had even tried hypnosis, acupuncture and nicotine gum. Nothing worked. But this time was different. This time I wanted to be happy. This time I wanted to feel good and be able to enjoy the rest of my life in good health. I wanted to stop worrying every day about all the smoking-related illnesses I was sure I would get.

I finally made a decision to be happy. I realized that I deserved to be happy as much as anyone else. My happiness was contingent on the quality of the rest of my life. The quality of the rest of my life was contingent upon stopping smoking.

I locked myself in the house so I couldn't run out to get cigarettes. I kept my mind busy by writing. I kept on shoveling food into my mouth. It was sheer hell. It was harder than anything I had ever done in my life. But I refused to give up no matter how many times I felt compelled to cheat. I kept telling myself that the physical discomfort that I would have to put up with temporarily in order to quit was much less than the excruciating agony that I would have to endure when I finally got cancer.

So I quit—not without cheating or gaining 10 pounds. But I did it. The result was not only looking and feeling better, but I now had a new sense of control over my life. I decided if I could stop smoking I could do anything—even overcome my genetic unhappiness!

But life wasn't about to make being happy that easy for me. One day I started feeling kind of flu-like. Then I got this horrible headache and couldn't move my neck from side to side. Then I started having these strange convulsions several times a day. I went to lots of doctors, none of whom knew what was wrong with me. One told me it was low blood sugar, another told me it was panic attacks, yet another told me that I was agoraphobic—one emergency room doctor handed me a prescription for Xanax and told me it was okay to leave on a ski trip, which I did. I almost died on that ski trip. It wasn't until we got back that I collapsed on the shower floor. The phone rang and I crawled out to answer it. It was a client whose husband was a doctor. I told her I needed help. It wasn't until I was hospitalized and they gave me a spinal tap that they realized I had been walking around all this time with viral spinal meningitis. My tactful neurologist told me, "Oh, I have another patient with the same thing. He just died." Anyway, through fate or strong will, here I am, still alive.

As if that weren't enough, the following year we went skiing in Utah. An out-of-control, possibly stoned, skier came plowing into me at full speed and knocked me down. His skis ran over my skis, causing me to twist and fall in such a way that I got a compound open fracture of my tibia and a hairline fracture of my fibula. I spent the next 10 days in the hospital in Utah having two surgeries to put a rod and screws through what was left of my tibia. When I got back to Los Angeles, the screws broke and I had to have a third operation to take them out.

Okay, I admit it—I'm a little accident prone. But the next "happening" was a shocker. I got up one morning, went to the bathroom, and I was urinating blood. "It's probably just a bladder infection," said a consoling girlfriend. *Right.* It turned out to be cancer of the ureter, a rare form of a high-grade bladder cancer. It came out of nowhere, but I learned later that smoking can cause bladder cancer.

Three doctors told me that they would have to remove one kidney, my ureter, and part of my bladder and that I must undergo chemotherapy. Determined not to lose my kidney, I found the only doctor in the world who could make me a new ureter from a piece of my intestines. So, within a week I underwent an eight-hour surgery and spent 10 days in the cancer ward of Norris Cancer Hospital at the University of Southern California. This wasn't fun, but my determination to be happy, my husband, and my good friends helped pull me through. I'm now cancer-free.

It was about the same time that my husband's auto salvage business started going bad. Not only did we lose the hundreds of thousands of dollars that we paid for it, but we kept on pouring our life's savings into it to keep it going. In hindsight, of course, this was a very poor decision. This was the beginning—and never the end—of our severe financial problems.

You'd think that about this time I'd just swallow a bottle of pills with a bottle of Vodka and call it quits. No, not I. I *chose* to be happy instead. I had the good fortune to be blessed with a sense of humor that allows me to see humor in the most traumatic of events. Although a sense of humor is usually genetic (my first cousin is comedienne Rita Rudner) you can still develop a sense of humor in how you deal with life.

You don't have to hurt inside anymore. You can *choose* to be happy or unhappy. You have the rest of your life left to live and you can *choose* to spend it dwelling on how miserable you are and on what you don't have, or you can *choose* to spend it with gratitude, enjoying what you do have. *It's your choice!*

Chapter 1

Why Am I So Unhappy?

It's 50% in Your Genes

The biggest obstacle to your happiness may be in your genes. Researchers have found that the tendency to be happy or unhappy is about 50% genetic. No matter how much good fortune you experience—you get that big house, big diamond ring, big promotion—in time the joy of your good fortune will fade and you will return to the "set-point" of happiness that you inherited.

In Scotland, researchers working with chronically depressed people identified a variation common among them in the gene that affects how the body handles serotonin, the brain's "feel-good" hormone. This discovery helps explain why depression runs in families.

Dr. Richard Davidson, Ph.D., a psychologist at the University of Wisconsin, used a brain imaging device to show that people differ radically in the amount of glucose that is burned in their brains. The more activity in the left frontal area of their brains, the happier and more enthusiastic they are. He also used an EEG in which he attached electrodes to a subject's scalp and measured which part gave off the most electricity. He proved that certain brains are predisposed to experience happiness more than other brains. His study concluded, "You are just born with it (happiness)."

At the University of Maryland, children as young as two days old were tested. They found that babies who smile a lot have more left frontal activity and that these patterns remain consistent as these children grow older. Arianna Shahanfahr, researcher, found that children come into this world with certain biological dispositions to display particular emotions.

Thomas Bouchard, Ph.D., a psychologist at the University of Minnesota, conducted studies that found that identical twins, whether raised together or apart, still share the same disposition. He writes, "If only environment shaped our personality, identical twins reared apart would have no similarity. And yet, they're every bit as similar as identical twins reared together. So, we're looking at about 50% effect of genetic influences."

David T. Lykken, a behavioral geneticist at the University of Minnesota, published results from a study of 1500 pairs of twins in *Psychological Science.* He states that "About half of your sense of well-being is determined by your 'set point,' which is from the genetic lottery and the other half from the sorrows and pleasures of the last hours, days or weeks." He also states that "Life circumstances such as salary, education or marital status predicted only 2% of the variation within each pair of twins. Those in prestigious positions or professions were not happier than those who went to work in overalls, nor were those who finished their Ph.D.s any happier than those who never completed eighth grade. You can predict happiness levels vastly better just by knowing the other identical twin's score." He also states, "Nearly every trait has genetic roots—shyness, aggression, happiness, depression, criminal behavior, even traditional values and religion."

Lykken stresses that environment also plays an important part in overall behavior and characteristics. Though research has shown a genetic link to the trait of happiness, a lack of that genetic component does not mean that you will be unhappy. He states that "We can still be happy even without a particular genetic endowment. A sensible lifestyle can help us bounce above our genetic set point."

Other experts agree that environmental influences and personal motivation go a long way in modifying our inherited traits.

"Happiness can be defined as our positive emotions minus our negative emotions," says Auke Tellegen, Ph.D., professor of psychology at the University of Minnesota, an associate of Lykken who has also done research on happiness, well-being and genes. According to Tellegen, "About 5% of well-being is attributable to genetics, but, in general, happiness depends on how we handle our emotions." He adds that "Genes provide us with the hardware for happiness, but the software comes from learning."

In Dr. Bouchard's study of genetically identical twins that were separated in infancy and raised apart, it was found that genetics has a strong influence on personality traits, leisure, vocational interests and even social attitudes. Adopted children tend to resemble their biological parents in personality more than their adoptive parents. Identical twins reared apart have personalities that resemble each other about as closely as identical twins reared together. Even traditionalism, a measure of social and religious conservatism, seems to be largely genetic in origin.

The study of behavioral genetics shows that the environment is one of the main routes by which genes affect the mind. Your experiences shape your intellectual and emotional development. An active, venturesome child has a greater variety of experiences than a more passive or timid one. This is called *reactive gene-environment correlation*. Parents with high IQs are likely to provide their offspring with greater intellectual stimulation as well as a genetic advantage. This is called *passive gene-environment correlation.* But most important is the *active gene-environment correlation*, which is your tendency to seek out experiences that are compatible with your genetic tendencies.

If you have diabetes or hypertension (both genetic conditions) you can control your sugar level and blood pressure with diet and exercise. If you have a genetic tendency to be overweight, you can be thin, but you must work much harder than a genetically-thin person must in order to be lean. In this same way, if you have a genetic tendency to be unhappy, you can overcome it by putting into practice the thought processes I've suggested in this book.

Just as a right-handed person who has had his right hand amputated is able to retrain his brain to use his left hand just as efficiently, a genetically unhappy person can retrain his mind to think like a happy, positive person by reprogramming his or her inner-thoughts.

If you think positive thoughts, you will bring happiness to yourself and if you think negative thoughts, you will bring unhappiness to yourself. Therefore, if you *choose* to be happy, you must learn to control your inner-thought processes by retraining them. Yes, you can even learn to reverse your negative inner thoughts to be positive, loving thoughts—thoughts I guarantee will bring you happiness. But first, you must decide that you *deserve* a happy life rather a life filled with hardship and misery. Your life is like one big interactive movie and *you* can control the events.

❧ *You possess the power to create your own happiness* ❧

G

Chapter 2

Happiness Is a Choice

You Are the Master of Your Own Destiny

Happiness is a state of mind. It is not something you possess. It is not the events in your life, but your *attitude* about the events in your life. It is not how much you have or achieve during your lifetime, but rather the quality of your journey through life. It is not the temporary "fix" of instant gratification. It is an inner peace. It is the act of loving yourself. It is the act of loving others despite their flaws. It is the act of loving mankind. It is always seeing the good in everyone and everything and overlooking the bad. It is the ability to forgive yourself and others for not being perfect. No other person can provide you happiness. You must *choose* to be happy in order to be happy.

Basic inner happiness or unhappiness is different than being happy or unhappy about something. We all experience events or have people in our lives that will temporarily make us happy or unhappy. However, this is happiness or unhappiness that we get over quickly. When we have a basic inner unhappiness it gnaws at us night and day, *every* day. It is like a nagging pain that overshadows the many good things that happen to us.

Perception

"How can I be happy when I have so many problems?" you ask. Because your happiness depends on your *perception* of your problems. Life seems to be one problem after another for all of us. We run the obstacle course and jump one hurdle after another, but the hurdles just keep on coming. Sometimes our problems pile up on top of each other and we feel so overwhelmed that all we feel like doing is climbing into bed and pulling the covers over our heads. But no matter how insurmountable *your* problems are or may seem, you can *choose* to be so distraught that you feel like committing suicide or you can see your problems as an exciting challenge and learning experience.

> ∾ *Happiness is a state of mind. It is not something you possess.*
> *It is not the events in your life,*
> *but your **attitude** about the events in your life* ∾

Accentuate the Positive

People who grew up in the fifties and sixties say "Life used to be easier," and that is probably true, but if you *choose* to be happy in a rapidly changing world, you must *accept* that some changes are good and some changes are bad. Regardless of whether the changes are good or bad, they are happening and there is not a darn thing you can do about it.

You can sabotage your happiness with anger over terrorism, drive-by shootings, or sex offenders being let out of prison, or you can learn to focus on all the wonderful children in our society who are achievers or the philanthropists who give all their money to cancer research. Always accentuate the positive and de-emphasize the negative.

Choose to be happy by trusting that life has a way of rewarding good and punishing evil. Life is ultimately just, but even when it doesn't seem to be, there is nothing you can do about it. Your job is to be happy and to serve mankind by making other people happy through your kindness, deeds and work.

You *Deserve* Happiness

Insist on your right to be happy. Don't let anyone try to sabotage your happiness—and believe me, there are those who will try. Life is a precious gift to be enjoyed, not a burden to be endured. If you are not happy, if you are not enjoying your life, *choose* to do something about it now.

In order to be happy you must first really believe that you *deserve* to be happy. Everyone deserves to be happy. The "pursuit of happiness" is your inalienable right. No one has the right to take that away from you. If a person makes you unhappy, he or she is toxic.

When my husband and I were planning our wedding we met with a rabbi. At that time each of our daughters—both teenagers—were making our lives miserable. We tried and tried to be good parents, but no matter how hard we tried, their behavior was intolerable. The rabbi told us, "No one, not even your children, has the right to make you unhappy."

We joined Tough Love, an organization that helps people find a way to manage very difficult children. In desperation, we finally took a stand and refused to let our children make us unhappy anymore. We refused to let them make us feel guilty for not giving them everything they demanded. We refused to feel guilty for not enjoying being with them. It is now many years later and our children are young adults. They have both apologized for making our lives so miserable and we have forgiven them because if we *choose* to be happy we *choose* to *forgive*. Had we not taken a stand against them making us unhappy, I doubt they would have grown up to be such wonderful young adults.

So, if anyone is making you unhappy, it is *your* fault for allowing that person to make you unhappy. If you are making yourself unhappy, then it is your fault you are unhappy. You are responsible for your own happiness.

Sometimes I pass a homeless person or someone who appears to be suffering and I feel guilty for being happy. Just because someone else is less fortunate than you does not mean that you are not deserving of the good fortune and happiness that is yours. It means that you should do what you can do to help others if you *choose* to do so, but that you should not allow your guilt over their misfortune to ruin your happiness. It is hard enough to solve your own problems without having to solve everybody else's problems.

This doesn't mean that you have to be insensitive to the plight of those less fortunate than you. If you have compassion for others you will feel good about yourself and thus enhance your own sense of well-being. Even selfless acts are selfish. I'm sure Mother Teresa got great pleasure from helping all the people she helped.

*By helping other people
you make yourself feel good about yourself.*

Chapter 3

Create Inner Peace

My husband took me to a Reba McEntire concert for my birthday a few years ago. I was sitting in the audience enjoying the magic of the live music, the bright lights, Reba's smile, the spirit of the people around me, and suddenly a wave of peaceful bliss came over me. For that moment I could see only good in the world. I was in an amphitheater that closed out the real world. Music filled the room with love and spirit. I felt no physical discomfort. I felt safe and secure. My worries vanished. It was then I realized that if you can create an environment for yourself where everything you see, hear, touch and smell bring positive thoughts—you can create your own sense of inner peace.

Feng Shui

The Chinese philosophy of Feng Shui practices living in harmony with nature and the physical landscapes of earth and awareness of the subtle energy lines in the environment. Good Feng Shui positioning creates harmonious relationships, good health, abundance, and prosperity. It creates a sense of well-being. Bad Feng Shui can bring illness, disaster, accidents, financial loss, unhappiness and even tragic death.

You don't have to believe in Feng Shui to walk into a home or office or building and feel "bad energy." In order to be healthy and happy it is important to live in a geographic environment that makes you feel good physically, mentally and emotionally. Whether you live in a single apartment or a huge house, fill your home with comfortable furniture, beautiful art, books, mementos from trips, and photographs that bring back good memories. Use candles, incense and herbal essences to create relaxing aromas and lighting. Play music you enjoy. Get rid of anything that you know is ugly or that makes you feel unhappy. (I suppose this could include a roommate, lover or spouse.)

Turn off the television and radio. Take your telephone off the hook. Throw out the newspaper. Close the doors and don't let in anything that will disturb your inner peace. This is your sanctuary.

Relax. Take a long bath. Listen to music. Read a good novel. Watch old re-runs of *I Love Lucy*. Work on an art project. Do anything you feel like doing. Refuse to let in the outside world. Refuse to feel guilty for enjoying your life. Practice finding inner peace and happiness whenever you can. The more you do it, the easier and more natural it becomes.

The "Wait 24 Hours Rule"

When I opened the mail yesterday I found that the bank had charged our business account a $27 non-sufficient funds fee because some $5 deduction had been automatically taken out of our account, which was $10 overdrawn. When I called the bank I spoke with a woman named Doreen, who was obviously suffering from PMS. I have spoken to Doreen on numerous occasions and I am sure she knows my name, but she kept on saying, "Listen, Ma'am." (I despise being called Ma'am.) I was agitated and ready to give her a piece of my mind, but I decided to follow my "Wait 24 Hours Rule" before acting or reacting.

I woke up this morning and all I wanted to do was write. I knew from experience that if I called Doreen at the bank, she would call me "Ma'am" again and tell me that the bank wasn't going to reverse the $27 charge. I would be aggravating myself and not doing what I really wanted to do, which was writing. The financial loss was $27. A visit to a good therapist to help me reduce the stress in my life would have cost me $150. Therefore, by accepting the injustice of the $27 non-sufficient funds charge, I saved $123!

*❧ If you **choose** to be happy,*
eliminate battles wherever and whenever feasible. ❧

The "Fifteen Percent Principle"

If you *choose* to be happy, *let go* of the injustices that have been done or you think have been done to you. In order to justify this passive-but-peaceful approach I always follow my "Fifteen Percent Principle." It means that in the process of living you will find that at least 15% of your after-tax money will go to:

- Interest, penalties and miscellaneous ridiculous charges from banks and credit card companies.
- Items you purchase that you find cheaper somewhere else later on.
- Items that you buy that you really didn't need.
- Items that break or fall apart.
- Clothes you can't fit into after the holidays.
- Health clubs you join and use once.
- Plumbing and automobile service "technicians" who perform unneeded repairs.
- Rude waiters and waitresses for whom you are too embarrassed not to leave a tip.
- Restaurant meals that were terrible.

The "Fifteen Percent Principle" also applies to people. Fifteen percent of:

- All drivers will flip you the bone if you honk at them.
- All government workers will slam down the window on you in order to take a lunch break even though you've been standing in line for four hours.
- The people you meet or date who say, "Let's have lunch" or "I'll call you" won't follow through.
- Your friends will forget your birthday.
- The people you know will come from dysfunctional families.
- Your friends will disappoint you at least once in your life.
- Other people's actions and reactions won't make sense.

If you accept and always remember my "Fifteen Percent Principle" you will eliminate the stress and aggravation that is guaranteed to rob you of more than 15% of your happiness.

Change Your Inner Dialogue

We are all having inner dialogue with ourselves 24 hours a day. Even while we are sleeping our brain is digesting all of the information it has absorbed during the day. Dreams are our body's way of sorting through and organizing the day's experiences in the same way a computer takes in vast amounts of information and stores it in different files.

People who dream every night are usually mentally healthier than people who do not dream, but if you don't remember your dreams it doesn't mean you don't dream. Just as your body feels heavy and lethargic if you haven't digested and eliminated yesterday's food properly, your brain can also get clogged with information and experiences that make you feel overwhelmed. And just as when you've eaten tainted food and end up sick, if your brain takes in too much polluted information and contaminated experiences, your mind ends up sick, too.

For example, during the Vietnam War many of our men experienced such horrific massacres and saw such pain and suffering that they suffer post-traumatic stress syndrome. A sound as simple as a click of a doorknob can make their mind think of the click of a trigger and they will relive the scene or scenes that haunt them over and over again.

Why did some men suffer post-traumatic stress syndrome and others come back to live perfectly normal lives with no negative psychological effects? Some brains have a better capacity than others to absorb information and experience, sort through it, and file away what it might need in the future, but "happy brains" are able to let go of those experiences that will in any way sabotage their future happiness.

We all experience some degree of post-traumatic stress syndrome and we all react to each new life experience based on past life experiences, but *how you digest* information and experiences is equally as important as what information and experiences you have. If you are a genetically happy person, you will usually take a negative experience and find a way to turn it into a positive experience. If you are a genetically unhappy person, you will usually take a negative experience and turn it into a major traumatic event or even a melodrama. After all, if you choose to go through life being unhappy, you need to find lots of reasons and excuses to be unhappy.

In order to turn your genetic unhappiness into chronic happiness, it is necessary to reprogram your negative inner dialogue into positive inner dialogue. You can't be happy at the same time you are having negative or mean thoughts. It is physically and mentally impossible.

Try to catch yourself every time you think a nasty thought. Always remind yourself that "I will always get back what I put out." Rephrase your thoughts to be positive and kind as often as you can. Never allow yourself to think a negative thought about yourself or anyone else. If you keep on doing this over and over again, eventually you will reprogram your brain to automatically think positive and kind thoughts.

Happy people usually feel as if other people really like them. If you want others to like you, you have to like yourself. And if you want to like yourself, you have to think positive, kind and compassionate thoughts. Think about it—would you like someone if you knew his or her thoughts were mean? Of course not. So how could you like yourself if you know your own thoughts are mean? You can't. If you *choose* to be happy you must change your negative inner thoughts.

Happiness and unhappiness are both life choices. People tend to choose what condition makes them feel the most comfortable. It has been found that many homeless people who are offered permanent shelter refuse it because they prefer to live on the streets because it is the only life they know and they are comfortable with it.

There was a story in the news a few years back about some private detectives that were searching for a man because he had inherited a million dollars and they wanted to give it to him. When they found him he was homeless and sleeping in a park. When he learned that he had inherited the money he told them he didn't want it. He ran away and disappeared, never to be found again.

Many unhappy people who are offered happiness either refuse it or find a way to sabotage it over and over again because they are uncomfortable being happy. Think of all the celebrities who achieve fame and fortune only to sabotage their success with drugs, alcohol or even suicide.

In order to stop sabotaging your own happiness, you must *choose* to embrace your newly-found happiness. Of course, there will be some voids in your life you will have to fill. You will have to find things to talk about other than your problems and how miserable you are. You will have to find something worthwhile to fill up all the time you used to spend complaining. You will have to find new, happier friends to take the place of the old miserable friends who disappear when you no longer want to participate in the "poor me" game with them.

An extensive compilation of studies was done by "happyologists" David G. Myers of Hope College in Michigan and Ed Diener of the University of Illinois. They charted the supposed facts and myths of happiness or "subjective well-being," which they define as "A preponderance of positive thoughts and feelings about one's life." Here are some of the conclusions published in an issue of *Psychological Science*:

- Knowing someone's age gives no clue to the person's average sense of well-being.
- Women tend to be miserable while men tend to be antisocial, but unhappiness is not gender biased.
- European Americans report only slightly more happiness than African Americans, who are slightly more prone to depression.
- An individual's unhappiness can stem from poverty and there is a correlation between a nation's wealth and its collective happiness. But these correlations are not universal. For instance, a study showed that the Irish were generally more satisfied than the richer folks in what was then West Germany. Only 32% of U.S. residents polled in 1993 said they were "very happy" as opposed to 35% in 1957 when the U.S. per-capita income was only one half as high.
- Happy people tend to like themselves. They feel that they have control over their lives and are optimistic and extroverted.
- Happy people have more friends and closer relationships.
- Happy people enjoy their work.
- Married people are happier as a rule than divorced, separated or otherwise single people.

According to a more recent Gallup poll, married adults at all income levels are more likely to report being happy than even the wealthiest unmarried adults. Money also makes a difference in this poll. About 72% of the respondents with incomes of $75,000 or higher reported being very satisfied with their personal lives as compared with only 36% of those with incomes of $30,000 or less.

Everyone's Perception of Happiness Is Different

Last Mother's Day my husband and I went on our yearly ritual to the cemetery to bring flowers to all of our dearly departed. As I placed flowers on my Aunt Dora's grave, my husband said, "It's too bad she had to live such an unhappy life."

Aunt Dora was never married, had very few friends, rarely traveled and lived rather reclusively. When she was 70 years old she was diagnosed with Alzheimer's disease. Before she lost her ability to speak, I asked her if she was happy. She said, "Oh, yes, I've had a very good life. I really enjoyed my life. I don't regret a thing."

I realized that my husband was judging Aunt Dora's happiness on his own concept of happiness, not hers. Aunt Dora was obviously happy because she had achieved her own *perception* of happiness.

It doesn't matter what you have or don't have or how exciting a life you live or don't live. If you think you're happy, you're happy, and, if you think you're unhappy, you're unhappy. Logically, then, the answer to being happy is to trick yourself into thinking that you're happy.

How? Sing, dance, work out or do anything except drink or take drugs, which only divert your attention away from your unhappiness. Try this experiment. Smile. Hold the smile and don't let it go. Now, think of the saddest thing you can think of and try to feel sad. Try to cry. But don't let go of the smile. Can't do it, can you?

Try another experiment. The next time you're feeling really sad, force yourself to go to a health club. Take a step, dance, aerobics or spinning class with fast, loud music while trying to focus on your misery. Can't do it either, can you?

Are Your Values Making You Unhappy?

№ᴜᴗ᷄ y has a right to judge your values and morals, and that includes me. However, no matter what your religious beliefs, there is a universal concept of good and evil. Chances are that if you have lied or cheated or hurt another living being you don't like yourself. If you don't like yourself, you certainly can't love yourself. And, if you don't love yourself, you certainly can't find inner peace and happiness. But if you live in harmony with your good values and morals, you will like yourself, love yourself, and eventually find inner peace and happiness.

The *secret* of true happiness does not lie in material objects or the immediate gratification of your needs. Studies of lottery winners show that within a year most say they are no happier than they were before they won. In fact, in many cases, these people become unhappy because friends and relatives don't want anything to do with them anymore if they won't share their winnings.

Of course, if you don't have enough money for food, shelter and clothing it is hard to find joy. But how many restaurants can you eat in? How big and grandiose a house can you build? How many dresses and suits can you have hanging in your closet? How many expensive pieces of jewelry can you hang from your body?

Researcher Jeffrey Fagin of St. John's University found that if you give three month old babies a mobile with three objects on it, most of them will like it. If you then give them a mobile with 10 objects on it and then try to get them to go back to the mobile with three objects on it, they lose interest and cry. Obviously, it's human nature to keep on wanting more and more.

The Amish, a small religious order in Pennsylvania that refuses to take part in the modern world, seem to be happier than most of us. Why? Debbie Stone of ABC interviewed an Amish woman who explained, "It's peace and joy . . . happiness comes from the Lord that he's going to take care of me . . . our home is heaven . . . you have lots of cousins, maybe 100 or 150, that would always be there to take care of you . . . security we probably take for granted . . . I guess we all like material things . . . but doing without something you've never had is not a sacrifice."

Genuine happiness occurs when you establish a bond to other living beings and give up the notion that someone or something outside of yourself can make you happy. True happiness occurs when you love yourself and practice daily honesty and integrity of your thoughts, actions and words. If you can go to sleep every night truly liking yourself, then you have already laid the basic foundation of your happiness.

In complete contrast to the Amish way of life, I live on the Westside of Los Angeles. This is an affluent society in which one's youth, beauty, home, car, clothes, jewelry, the school which our children attend, the restaurants we frequent and the trips we take are all measures of our success. This, we all realize, is an inaccurate measurement of our real self-worth, but we all use it as a yardstick anyway.

In the early 1990's, a recession had been in progress for several years. The real estate market had plummeted and many people who were worth multimillions were living in single apartments trying to make enough money just to eat. Doctors were complaining that they were no longer making four and five hundred thousand dollars a year. They were forced to accept whatever Medicare and the health insurance companies were willing to pay them. Attorneys were still charging exorbitant fees, but they were unable to collect them. These were very sobering and humbling years for many people. Those who learned the lessons this recession had taught them emerged happy in spite of it all.

On Black Monday in 1929 when the stock market crashed, people jumped out of the windows when they learned that they had lost all of their money. How sad that these people's happiness was based on the value of their portfolios. (By the way, if these people just waited out the stock market instead of committing suicide, they would be billionaires today.)

In yet another contrast, I am reminded of the survivors of The Holocaust. As they lay starving in concentration camps they had to find a reason to survive in order to survive. They had nothing and yet they were able to find happiness in a morsel of food. The lesson here? Everything in life is relative.

> *Your happiness and how you survive adversity depends on one thing—your **attitude**.*

Dreams and Fantasies

Dreams are just dreams. Whether or not you fulfill your fantasies is sometimes not up to you. If you have done everything in your power to fulfill your dreams, you are successful. If you *choose* to be happy, you must *choose* to believe that everything happens for a reason and that every event will turn out to affect you positively in the long run, even if you *never* achieve your dreams.

Problem Solving 101

Problems have a way of stacking up on top of each other like dirty clothes piling up on a bed. Sometimes that pile of dirty clothes becomes so overwhelming that you lose the energy and drive needed to tackle it and you end up succumbing to lethargy and helplessness.

If you *choose* to be happy, *choose* to see each of your problems as yet another challenge to overcome. Solve each problem one by one just as you would wash and hang up each article of clothing neatly in the closet, one at a time. Eventually, the bed will be cleared of all of the dirty clothes and you can climb under the covers and finally get some well deserved rest.

All problems have solutions. Some solutions you may not like, but they are solutions nonetheless. Sometimes you just need to step away from your problems in order to come up with a solution. It's like when you try over and over again to reconcile your checkbook, but keep on getting more and more frustrated each time you try again and can't do it. If you put it away for a day, the next day you can usually reconcile it easily. My "Wait 24 Hours Rule" applies to *all* of your problems.

Sometimes your problems have a way of solving themselves. Have you ever noticed that often when you are just relaxing and reading the information you've been looking for miraculously pops up? Or, you need something done and you inexplicably meet someone that day that can help you?

Life has a remarkable way of sending you all the answers, sources and solutions you need if you just relax and stay "in sync" with the Universe and put out "happiness vibes."

How to Make New Friends

Speaking of "happiness vibes," I recently met Yvonne, a young girl who complained to me that she was miserable because she had no friends. I said "Maybe you have no friends because you are emitting 'unhappiness vibes'." It's no secret that happy, successful people want to surround themselves with other people who are also happy and successful. And *all* people want to be around other people who are happy and make them laugh and feel good about themselves.

"But it's impossible to put on a happy face when I work so hard all the time and I always have a headache," Yvonne complained to me.

"Maybe you have no friends because you complain too much," I suggested.

Of course, this is not to say that no one will want to be friends with you if you have problems. All people have problems and feel better if they can discuss them with their friends. That's what friends are for. But you shouldn't *harp* on your problems. Ask for your friends' opinions and advice, listen carefully and then move on. Don't bore people with your same problems over and over again. Speaking of bores, I know a man at my health club—let's call him Jason—who can clear a room faster than a leper with chickenpox. Jason has no friends because he is a bore. He reads airplane manuals from cover to cover and loves to show off his photographic memory by reciting statistics.

If you want to make new friends, be entertaining and motivating. Meet new people by offering them a compliment—perhaps their hair, perfume, shoes—anything that makes them feel good about themselves and opens up a conversation.

Wendy inadvertently (or purposely, who knows?) makes other people feel bad about themselves. Nobody likes criticism or backhanded compliments. If making people feel bad is the only way you know how to make yourself feel good about yourself, you are sabotaging your own happiness.

There is no shortage of happiness. Making someone else happy will only increase your own "happiness bank." The more happiness you have in your "happiness bank," the more happiness you will have to give others.

Tracey has no friends because she is totally self-absorbed. She chatters incessantly about herself. If you try to interrupt and say something about yourself, she will not listen and just talk right through you. If you want more friends, stop focusing on yourself so much. Ask people about themselves, their work, their life, their family and their feelings. Listen carefully when others speak. Have compassion for their problems instead of bending their ears with your own problems. People love to talk about themselves—especially those who haven't read this book *yet*. (Maybe you should give them a copy?)

Be well-rounded—and no, I don't mean your body shape. Take an avid interest in what is happening in the world. Talk about other things beside yourself. Maybe even find a favorite charity.

Leslie, who has just been dumped by her boyfriend, complained to me recently "I'm unhappy because I'm so lonely."

"Maybe you're lonely because you are so unhappy," I suggested. Nobody wants to be with someone who is desperate. Nobody wants to be with you just because you are lonely and need someone to be with. People are not dumb. They know when you are using them to cure your loneliness.

My mother was always very lonely after my father passed away. She complained about being lonely and depressed to everyone all the time. It was like a broken record. Even the most compassionate of my mother's friends didn't want to spend their lives listening to her complain about how lonely and depressed she was. And so eventually what people she did have left in her life didn't want to be with her. Her inability to create a fulfilling life for herself created even more loneliness. Loneliness is a catch-22. Feeling lonely makes you feel unhappy. Feeling unhappy makes you lonely.

I don't want to sound callous. I do know firsthand that loneliness is very painful. When I was first going through my divorce I used to sit at home at night sipping on wine, writing poetry and crying. Many times I considered suicide. I would fantasize about being found dead in my bed. I would look incredibly beautiful draped in the most expensive peignoir set I could find at Neiman Marcus. Who cares about paying the bill after you're dead, right?

Then, luckily, my sense of humor would surface. I'd say to myself, "My luck, I won't commit suicide successfully and I'll end up a vegetable, not to mention having to pay the bill from Neiman Marcus for the peignoir set." I gave up that fantasy when I read somewhere that when you overdose on pills you turn blue and blow up.

But Sunday afternoons were the loneliest. I would watch couples and families having a good time throwing Frisbees in the park. It seemed like everyone had a mate but me. That was an extremely lonely, painful time in my life. So, I do know how painful loneliness can be. What I didn't know then was how not to be lonely. So, let me share what I've learned since then.

If you want to conquer your loneliness you have to get past focusing solely on yourself. You must stop believing that if you are only half of a couple, you are not a whole person. You need to stop believing that only the perfect mate can cure your loneliness. Remind yourself that there are many people with mates who are lonelier than if they were by themselves. You are born alone and you die alone and only *you* can fulfill your own needs. Nobody knows what it feels like to live inside your skin. Focus on the world outside of yourself and stop dwelling on your loneliness and everything else will fall in place.

❧ *You are your own soul mate* ❧

Shelly is a woman in her mid-fifties who was married only briefly many years ago and has been alone most of her life raising her two children by herself. She confessed to me recently, "I feel so lonely that there's a constant ache in my soul." It tore my heart apart.

And yet Shelly, who yearns so deeply for a life companion, refuses to go after what she wants. She's bitter and cynical because life hasn't given her what she wants. She sees herself as a victim. She gets herself all dolled up and goes to bars to find men. Well, of course, there aren't too many quality men hanging out at singles bars looking for middle-aged women. She refuses to see what she is doing to create her own loneliness and unhappiness.

On the other side of the coin, I was at a dinner party the other night and the lovely couple seated next to us confessed that they had met 15 months ago through an online dating service. Here were two people who had successfully taken a pragmatic approach to finding the right mate.

Asserting control over your life and your destiny instead of declaring yourself a victim of life is essential to your feelings of self-worth. Having a good sense of your self-worth is essential to your happiness.

Instigate an aggressive course of action to pump up your "happiness bank." Join groups, organizations, a gym, take classes, go anywhere you think the type of people you would like to meet would most likely be. Put on a smile whether you feel like it or not. Start conversations by complimenting others. Be proactive! I promise that you will get back exactly what you put out, which brings me to ...

Like Attracts Like

It's a basic law of nature—if you put out a smile, you'll get back a smile. If you are a good friend, you'll attract good friends. You get back what you put out. *It never fails.*

Did you ever notice that on the days that you feel happy and up that everyone else seems to be happy and up, too? No coincidence. They are feeling your good mood and returning it to you. Everyone loves to be around a smiling happy person and hates to be around a miserable person.

"But how can I exude happiness when I feel so miserable inside?" Leslie complained to me.

"Pretend" I told her. "Try an experiment tomorrow. When you get up in the morning and no matter how depressed you feel, no matter how miserable you think your life is, make believe you are the happiest person in the world. Pretend you feel and look great. Think only good thoughts about everyone and everything that you encounter, as hard as it may be."

"But that's being a phony!" she screamed at me.

"Yes, and at first you will feel like a phony," I told her. "But walking around with a smile on your face is going to bring better results than walking around with a scowl on your face. Eventually your smile will affect the way people respond to you, and then your smile will not be phony."

"But it's too hard to hide my loneliness," she whined.

"Just *pretend* you're not lonely. Direct your attention to matters outside of yourself. Take cooking classes. Become an animal rights activist. Do anything that distracts your attention from yourself and your misery. Miraculously, you will feel better."

∾ *That which you dwell on will become a reality.*
If you dwell on your loneliness, you will become lonelier.
If you dwell on your happiness, you will become happier. ∾

Practice Harmlessness of Thoughts, Words and Actions

When you get up every morning, say to yourself, "I am going to practice harmlessness of thoughts, actions and words today." If, during the day, you catch yourself thinking negative or malicious thoughts—stop! If you find yourself doing something that is not nice—stop! *Mean people cannot be happy people.*

"But what if I encounter someone who isn't nice to me? Am I supposed to think good thoughts about that person?" a happiness-resistant friend asked me.

"Yes!" I said. "Tell yourself that person who just cut you off in traffic, flipped you the bone, and tossed the milkshake out the window that hit your windshield is only a product of his or her environment. That person only did such a despicable act because of his or her own self-esteem problems. Feel sorry for that person for being so angry. He must not be very happy inside. If you are compassionate about that person's problems, you will feel good about yourself."

"Try another experiment," I told her. "Act really nice to any person you encounter who is particularly aloof or nasty. Be as sweet as you can to her. Start a conversation. Give a compliment. She will usually be incredibly receptive to your friendliness. You've probably mistaken her aloofness for her inner feelings of poor self-esteem and sadness. People who really feel good about themselves are usually warm and friendly."

Purpose

"I am unhappy because I have no purpose," said a friend of mine who had just lost her husband. For the past 25 years her life had revolved around her husband. She had been taking care of him—cooking him gourmet meals, making lavish dinner parties, keeping their home spotless and catering to her husband's every need. "I have nothing to get out of bed for" she confessed to me with tears in her eyes.

I was reminded of how I used to visit my mother, my aunt and my father-in-law in their nursing homes every week before they passed away. I watched as they and the other patients deteriorated month after month. They sat around day after day, night after night, with nothing to do, apathetic, waiting to die. They had no obstacles to overcome, no hurdles to jump, no challenges to meet. They had no reason to get up in the morning. There were no efforts. There were no rewards. This is when I realized that it is the challenge of jumping the hurdles of life that keeps us vital and alive. And it is feeling vital and alive that makes us happy.

If you say to yourself, "I'd be happy if I could just solve all my problems," you are wrong. You would sit back, relax and marvel at how perfect your life is—for about a day or two. And then you would say "What's next?" So you would go out looking for stress and problems because you were so totally bored with your life.

Joann married Arthur, a lovely man who had retired years ago with multimillions in the bank. They live a fairytale life, jetting between their homes in the South of France, Palm Beach, and the Upper Eastside of New York. They entertain their friends elegantly. They travel first class. Her wardrobe and jewelry are fabulous. They have enough money to go anywhere and do anything. One day she told me that they were starting a small business.

I asked her "What for?"

She said, "I just want to have something to do."

Most of us are not born with a *raison d'être*. In the process of growing up, most of us find one or more activities that we truly enjoy sooner or later. Stephen Spielberg found his passion in filmmaking early in life. Grandma Moses found her passion for painting very late in life.

If you don't have a reason to be, find one! It doesn't have to be permanent. It doesn't have to be grandiose. You can always change it.

Most of us would like to think that there is a deep meaning to life itself—that there is a purpose to our own lives and that we were put here for a reason. Yet, few of us know what that purpose is. We envy those who have found their passion in life.

*❧ If you **choose** to be happy, never go to bed at night without creating an exciting reason to wake up to in the morning. ❧*

Feeling "Stuck"

Are you unhappy because you feel "stuck" or "trapped" in an unexciting and unfulfilling life? Sometimes life is like one big traffic jam. Everyone is honking at each other and screaming obscenities out the window, but everyone refuses to move their car. Then suddenly one car moves an inch, the next car is able to maneuver out of the traffic jam, then, the next, and finally the traffic is flowing again. When you feel stuck, one tiny action can be just the catalyst you need to make your life flow again.

You're stuck in a job you can't stand because you can't afford to quit. You're stuck with a mate who bores you to tears but you can't afford to leave and besides, your mate has convinced you that no one would want you anyway. You're fat and you're ugly and you feel like throwing up every time you look in the mirror. Your credit card bills have mounted up and you can't even afford the minimum payment so how can you afford to leave your mate or your job?

You can't afford not to do it. There is nothing more precious than your life and your happiness. You've only been given one life. No more. No less. If you are stuck in an unhappy situation, change it. *Only you have the power to make yourself happy!*

Are You Causing Your Own Unhappiness?

If you are reading this book it is obvious that you feel unhappy at least some of the time if not all of the time. If you really want to be happy, it will serve you well to identify exactly what in your life is making you unhappy.

» Do you feel something or someone is missing in your life?

» Do you feel like you are not part of life? That you are on the outside looking in?

» Do you feel that life is passing you by?

» Do you feel your life has no meaning?

» Are you afraid you will wake up one day and be too old to enjoy your life?

» Do you hate your life?

» Do you hate yourself?

» Are you constantly struggling with feelings of jealousy?

» Do you hate everybody and everything?

» Are you constantly searching for answers?

» Are you always looking for someone or something to make you happy?

» Do you call or go to astrologers or psychics in hope that they will tell you something good will happen to you?

» Do you go to a therapist and rehash your childhood and your relationships over and over again?

» Is another person making you unhappy?

» Is your job making you unhappy?

» Is your poor self image making you unhappy?

» Is lack of money making you unhappy?

» Do you think of yourself as a failure?

» Is nothing you do good enough?

» Are your fears sabotaging your enjoyment of life?

» Are you feeling overwhelmed by life?

» Do you worry obsessively?

» Do you feel numb?

» Are you walking around in a daze?

» Do you have episodes of sadness and crying?

» Do you feel guilty?

» Do you feel distracted and unable to concentrate?

» Do you forget things?

» Are you preoccupied with the past and what could have or might have been?

» Are you obsessed over a loss?

» Do you daydream?

» Do you have nightmares?

» Do you go over and over your problems in your head?

» Are you always tired?

» Do your arms and legs feel heavy?

» Do you have panic attacks?

» Have you lost your appetite?

» Do you have insomnia?

» Do you have surges of energy?

» Do you get some kind of satisfaction out of being unhappy?

» Do you feel most comfortable when you are unhappy?

» Do you feel frustrated?

» Do you feel anxious?

» Do you feel resentful?

» Are you indecisive?

» Are you self-critical?

If you answered "yes" to even one of these questions, reading this book will definitely help you improve the quality of your life. You are causing your own unhappiness by focusing on what is wrong with your life instead of focusing on what is *right* with your life.

*❧ The problem is within **you**.*
*Therefore, the answer must be within **you**.❧*

Chapter 4

Let Go!

If you *choose* to be happy you have to let go of old hurt and pain and accept change. Change is an integral part of life that moves it forward. From birth until death all living cells are constantly changing. If you resist change you resist growth as nature intended it. And if you aren't growing and changing, you can't truly be happy.

Let Go of Negative Behaviors

We all cling to familiar behavior that keeps on creating negative results over and over again just because we are comfortable with that behavior and we fear change. It is too much of a threat to our self-esteem to admit that we could be doing something wrong. But when you let go of your old negative behavior your life will automatically get better.

Most of us have one or more undesirable personality traits. When these little quirks and idiosyncrasies escalate into negative behaviors that cause us to lose jobs and alienate our friends and family, it's time to change our behavior because it is sabotaging our happiness. We can defend our behavior and our right to express ourselves all we want, but when it is affecting our lives negatively we need to change it if we *choose* to be happy.

Nora is a hypochondriac. She knows that she gets the attention she craves from being sick all the time or having accidents, so she is always sick or having accidents. These illnesses and accidents create very convenient excuses for not working or doing something productive with her life. She is a master of finding enablers who have much sympathy for her ill fortune. But most people get tired of her complaining sooner or later. When someone gets fed up with hearing about her misery, she promptly extricates him or her from her life and moves on to the next victim of her victimization.

If you are unhappy, you probably keep on doing the same thing over and over again even if it gets bad results. You proclaim yourself "unlucky" or a "victim." In contrast, happy people take notice when they keep on doing the same thing over and over again and always get bad results. They ask themselves and others, "What is it that I am doing to create these bad results?" They really want to know the answer. They accept the answer as truth. They make the behavioral changes they need to make.

Let Go of Negative Attitudes

Let go of old attitudes that are making you unhappy. Your attitude about what happens to you while you are going through the process of living is partially genetic and partially learned in early childhood. If you were born to genetically unhappy parents, chances are the attitudes you learned from them are negative. If you *choose* to be happy, it's time to let go of the old attitudes that are sabotaging your happiness.

Most of us are so used to thinking the way we think that we really don't even realize that our attitudes are negative. In order to determine whether you have a negative or positive attitude ask yourself the following two simple questions:

» Do I feel happy and energized most of the time? If you answered "yes," you have a positive attitude.
» Do I feel unhappy and miserable most of the time? If you answered "yes," you have a negative attitude.

Rewrite Your Inner Dialogue

Each time you feel sad, write down what you are thinking. It will always be a negative thought. For instance, I was just thinking that the pain in my neck is really hurting me and giving me a terrible headache. I just don't know how I'm going to go through the rest of my life in this pain, let alone finish writing this book.

Now that I've written it down I can see what a self-defeating negative attitude this is. So, I'll reword it. My neck is acting up so I think I'll take a break from writing, take an anti-inflammatory and a hot bath

so I'll feel better, and then I'll come back and continue writi.
hope will be a bestselling self-help book. *Much more positive, ̗gnt?*

Make a habit of writing down your negative thoughts and then re-writing them as positive statements. The more often you do this, the more effective you will be in reprogramming your inner dialogue to be happier. Stop being a victim of your own negative emotions by creating your own negative self-fulfilling prophecies. If you go to sleep every night thinking about what misfortunes will happen to you tomorrow, you will most likely wake up to misfortune. But, if you go to sleep each night thinking about what wonderful things are going to happen to you the next day, you will wake up to a day filled with wonderful, positive surprises. That's because life has this fabulous way of giving you what you want.

Let Go of Your Past

Live in the now. The past is gone and you can't do anything about it. Hopefully, you have already learned from it. The future is always one step away, so you can never experience it. There-fore, the only time you have on this earth is right now. Learn to enjoy it.

Let go of the old to make room for the new. Have you ever refused to clean out your closet because you thought that if you got rid of everything that's old and worn out or out of style or that you knew you would never wear again, your closet would be empty? But when you finally brought yourself to clean out your closet, it miraculously filled up again with newer, more stylish clothes?

Cleaning out your mind is similar. Get rid of old thoughts, ideas and people that are no longer an asset to your life. At first, you will feel a void. But slowly, your life will start filling up with new, more positive ideas, thoughts and people.

Stop Passing the Blame

In order to get up the courage to let go of your past it is necessary to stop blaming others for your unhappiness and failures. This means you will have to take responsibility for your failures without the luxury of blaming it on your parents or an ex-spouse or your third grade teacher. If you *choose* to be happy from this moment forward, use your newly-found energy to take positive action to create a more optimistic, happy future.

Did you ever notice that when something bad happens or someone says something that is bothering you, you obsess with thoughts of that incident? Then you talk it out with your best friend or your mate and after rehashing it over and over again you are finally able to let it go.

The same theory works on bad memories. Talk about bad memories that are bothering you with someone you trust or just write them down. Do this only until you are satisfied that you better understand what happened. Dispose of any residue that reminds you of that bad memory and then release that bad memory. Forgive those who might have wronged you. That is the past. This is the here and now. Whatever happened happened. You can't change it.

Next, replace the bad memory with a good memory. Perhaps it was when you were little and your mother baked brownies and you got to lick the bowl. Talk only about good memories. When a bad memory pops into your head, exorcise it immediately by replacing it with a good memory. The more you practice this the better you will become at it.

When my mother was 70 years old she started showing signs of Alzheimer's disease but I didn't realize it. I was totally confused about her bizarre personality changes. She was getting increasingly confused and I had to do more and more for her. She wanted me to take her to a car dealership to buy a new car. (Yes, I cringe at the fact that she was still driving. It wasn't until later when she asked me, "Which is the gas pedal and which is the brake pedal?" that I realized the magnitude of her impairment.) Anyway, I spent a complete day taking her from car dealership to car dealership, enduring much embarrassment as she called all the salesmen "crooks" to their faces and shouted "You're trying to cheat me" to them. Needless to say, she didn't buy a car that day.

The next morning she called me and shouted, "What kind of daughter are you? You won't even take me shopping for a car!"

I said, "Mother, I spent all day yesterday with you."

She screamed back, "No you didn't!"

A few months later I discovered that she hadn't been paying her bills correctly. A part of her realized that she was not able to do things right anymore, and so she put my name on her bank account so that

I could take care of her financial affairs. She seemed grateful that I would do this for her.

The next morning I got a call from the police who were at her house. She had actually called the police and accused me of stealing all of her money! Imagine how hurt I felt.

But the behavior that devastated me the most were the months of angry phone calls all night long in which she called and screamed, "Drop dead you bastard daughter!" into my answering machine

The next morning I would call and explain to her that I was just trying to help her. I had let my design business go and would spend each day taking her to doctors and wherever else it was she wanted to go. But that night the same pattern would begin again. The abusive phone calls came all night long. I can't tell you how hard I cried and how devastated I was. I tried so hard to help my mother and she treated me so cruelly. And yet, I had to continue to take care of her, as there was no one else to do it.

It is now years later and I clearly understand what Alzheimer's disease can do to one's mind. I have learned to forgive my mother for how badly she had hurt me. First, because if I didn't, I knew I couldn't be happy. Second, I knew intellectually that this behavior was stemming from a severe mental disease.

Nora can't let go of the fact that her father was verbally abusive when she was growing up. He had always wanted a son and was so disappointed that she was born a female that he tried to make her feel that nothing she ever did was good enough. Nora says she loves her father dearly but can't seem to do anything that pleases him. She has many physical ailments and an apparent eating disorder. Recently she said she had to get up and leave a movie in the middle because it reminded her of how badly her father treated her when she was growing up. "Why can't he just be proud of me?" she asks.

If Nora *chooses* to be happy, she has to let go of the fantasy that her father will someday tell her how proud of her he is. If she doesn't accept that she just can't change how *he* thinks and acts, she will never find happiness. Her symptoms will persist. Nora needs to forgive him, let go of her anger, and change the way *she* thinks and acts.

❧ You can't change another human being, you can only change the way you perceive what they say and do. ❧

Isn't it ridiculous to think that your happiness is based on what one person who happens to be your genetic parent thinks of you? Isn't it a lot wiser to base your feelings of self-worth on what you think of yourself and what positive feedback you get from all your wonderful accomplishments and relationships?

I am reminded of some of the demeaning comments my mother used to make to me, like, "Did you mean for your hair to look like that?" I was very young and insecure and these comments were far from complimentary. However, in hindsight, I am now wise enough to consider the source—a depressed woman with a history of mental illness and shock treatments.

Always consider the source. If someone is always trying to make you feel bad about yourself, take a good look at that person's motives and mental health. Nobody with good motives and good mental health would purposely say or do anything that would make you feel bad about yourself. If these people were happy and mentally healthy, they would want you to be happy, too. If anyone says or does something that hurts you, it's because of his own shortcomings, not yours. He is unhappy because he has negative thoughts that cause him to behave negatively towards you. Have compassion because he is unhappy and cannot see the correlation between his own negative thoughts and behavior and his own unhappiness.

One of the signs of true happiness is the sincere desire for others to be happy, too. If a person is truly happy and mentally stable, he will do everything in his power to make you feel good about yourself.

Let go of the people who have caused you hurt and pain in the past. You can't change what has already happened. You can't change their thought processes, but you *can* change your own thought processes. See those experiences as learning opportunities. Use the lessons you have learned to improve the quality of your present and future life.

Let Go of Preconceived Ideas

Let go of inflexible ideas about how you think your life should be. We all have preconceived scenarios of how our lives should have been, but if you *choose* to be happy you must accept your life as it is right now. And if who you are is not quite as glamorous as who you read about in the tabloids and magazines and see on television and in the movies, remind yourself that you don't live inside that person's skin. You don't know what she feels. You don't know what pain she suffers. You don't *really* know whether she is happy or unhappy. If you *choose* to be happy, count your blessings every day.

Remember the first time we all saw Princess Diana walk down the aisle at her fairytale wedding? Her beauty, wealth, popularity and lifestyle were enviable. But here was a woman who was dreadfully unhappy a good deal of the time. She eventually learned that she could find happiness in doing for others that were less fortunate than she. She was quoted as saying, "The sun is finally coming up in my life again" when she embarked on her tragically short relationship with Dodi Fayed.

Your happiness is not your life scenario. It is not what you have achieved in your career or what you look like or what you own or how popular you are. Your happiness is what you feel inside every day when you wake up in the morning. It doesn't matter whether you are a celebrity and make 20 million dollars a movie or you are working at Taco Bell for minimum wage. It doesn't matter whether you are President of the United States or a bus driver. It is what you feel and what you think that makes you happy.

Let Go of the Need To Be Right

What difference does it make whether you are right or wrong? If you *choose* to be happy, let go of the need to prove anything to anyone—including yourself.

Let Go of Your Past Mistakes

Stop beating yourself up! You made every decision in your life the best way you knew how to given the information you had to work with at the time. Sometimes your decisions were right. Sometimes they were wrong. Sometimes sheer luck kicked in. Sometimes bad luck cursed you. Sometimes you made good decisions that turned out bad for reasons beyond your control. If you don't make any decisions because you are afraid of making a mistake you will be *stuck*.

Decisions are part of every day life. Some are small, some are big. All you can do is weigh the facts, learn everything you can about the subject, and make the best decision you can. If you are wrong, then you are wrong. That doesn't make every decision you are going to make in the future wrong. It only makes that one decision wrong. Keep on making the wisest decisions you can make. Some of them are bound to end up right.

Nolan is beating himself up constantly for not making the right investment decisions. He could have bought IBM stock when it was low. He could have bought a condo in a location where values appreciated instead of depreciated. He dwells on what he did wrong and never seems to mention what he does right. But, as we know, like attracts like. If he focuses on being wrong and sees himself as always having bad luck, he's going to attract bad luck. Nolan is comfortable being a victim and a loser and so he subconsciously puts himself in that position. When I mention this to him, he agrees with me. But he doesn't change it. Don't give in to the "with my luck" trap. Change your mindset about yourself, your luck and your life.

Let Go of Obsessive Thoughts

Most of us are plagued by obsessive thoughts that sabotage our happiness. I used to obsess over money, or, more accurately, the lack of it. I spent every waking hour worrying about our mounting credit card debt, how we were going to make our house payment, and what we were going to live on when we retire, but the more I worried the worse the lack of money became. So, since worrying wasn't helping, I decided to just let go of it and give the problem over to our Higher Spirit. Unfortunately our Higher Spirit wasn't an accountant or a business manager, but at least I stopped obsessing over money and used my "worry energy" to do something about it.

Other people obsess over their health, how many calories they put in their bodies, or the spider veins on their thighs. Obsessing over something doesn't make the problem go away—it just makes you unhappy.

Obsessing over acts of Mother Nature such as earthquakes,

hurricanes and tornadoes is also a waste of time. Make your house and workplace as safe as you can, buy insurance, and then refuse to worry.

Obsessing over finding the perfect mate is also counterproductive. First of all, there is no such thing as the perfect mate. Everyone has human flaws. Obsessing makes you desperate and being desperate makes you vulnerable. You will get hurt. Get on with your life. Do the things you enjoy—alone, if you have to. Stop thinking that only another person can make you happy. The truth is that no one is going to give you inner happiness. A mate can share time with you and make you feel loved, but if you don't love yourself first, it won't matter. You will still be unhappy.

Let Go of Thoughts of Revenge

The old adage "living well is the best revenge" is the ideal way to deal with your obsessions over real or imagined slights. Helena used to see herself as a victim of her ex-husband who became extremely wealthy 24 hours after she signed their property settlement. She was so upset that she kept wishing that he would lose all his money. She said that she visualized herself driving by him in her brand new Bentley. He'd be a homeless guy standing on a street corner with one of those cardboard signs and she would just look at him and smirk. But thoughts of revenge are negative and toxic and will make you unhappy.

Let Go of "I Should Have"

Hindsight is always better than foresight. But, of course, you're not psychic. You had no way of knowing. If psychics were really psychic they wouldn't have to bother giving readings because they'd be so rich from playing the stock market. Stop beating yourself up for missing an opportunity. Use the same time and energy to find new opportunities. *It's never too late.*

Mindy keeps on saying, "I should have stayed in school and gotten a good education." Well, Mindy, if you didn't, you didn't, so stop beating yourself up. You weren't ready, willing and able to get a higher education at that time. Maybe you are now. It's never too late to go back to school. If you want something that badly, you'll find a way to get it.

Rachael keeps on saying, "I should have married someone else."

Perhaps you should have, Rachael, but when you got married you had plenty of good reasons why this was a good choice for a life partner. If things didn't work out the way you would have liked them to, don't beat yourself up. You made the best decision you could at that time." If you are unhappy in your marriage, find a way to change it or end the relationship.

Okay, so you promised to love your mate "for better or for worse, in sickness and in health." Morally and ethically, you have made a serious commitment and should stick by your commitment. However, if your mate has changed, or if you have changed, and this relationship is no longer making you happy, perhaps it's time to rethink your commitment to each other.

Let go of "I should have been born . . . (rich, beautiful, talented)" and work hard to create the "you" that you have always wanted to be. Fortunately, you were born in a time and place that allows you to grow and improve if you *choose* to put in the time and energy. Opportunities abound. You can change the way you look with cosmetic surgery, hair dye, exercise, make up and clothing. You can change your economic future by getting an education and working hard. You can social climb if you're so inclined. Granted, there are limitations. If you are a midget you're not going to be a runway model. But with hard work you can change your looks and your lifestyle if that is what will make you happy.

But remember, *you* are always *you* underneath. Unless you work on your inside as well as your outside, you will always feel like an imposter.

Chapter 5

Set Yourself Free

Fearful personalities are genetic. "The study of fear in animals such as mice has shown that fear can be selectively bred into succeeding generations, suggesting a strong genetic component," says William R. Clark, professor emeritus in the department of molecular, cell and developmental biology at the University of California at Los Angeles. "There is considerable evidence in humans, derived largely from studies of adopted children, and identical and fraternal twins reared together and apart, that a tendency toward anxiety and fear is an inheritable trait."

People who suffer anxiety attacks come from families with histories of anxiety attacks. Some people have such intense fears that they develop phobias such as fear of people, animals, natural phenomena, diseases, situations and activities. There are people who have so many fears that they become agoraphobic and never leave their homes. "Phobias with specific associations, such as snakes, fear of pain, or of heights or closed spaces are entirely associated with individual environmental experiences, but the tendency to develop fearful or anxious responses to the environment in general has a clear genetic component," says Clark.

Fears can also be manifested as obsessive-compulsive disorder. Some people are so afraid of germs that they wash their hands constantly and never touch a doorknob. Leslie will never go to the toilet in a public bathroom because she fears germs. She never goes on vacations or leaves home for any length of time. She has cheated herself out of most of the pleasurable experiences of life because of her fears. In many cases, obsessive-compulsive disorder has been found to have a chemical origin in the brain and can be successfully treated with a combination of drugs and therapy.

So why are other people so fearless? What makes a person become a stuntman? What makes a person want to go skydiving? It's the rush of adrenaline that the fear produces that gives him pleasure. It has also been scientifically proven that there are distinct differences in the brains of people who enjoy danger and the brains of people who have fears.

Let's assume you have normal fears. Most people are afraid of going to the dentist, flying in an airplane or having an operation. Since it's impossible to get through life without one or more of these experiences, how do we get rid of these fears?

Most fears are founded on ignorance and dread of the unknown. Once you finally force yourself to do something that you have always feared you will be amazed at how painless it really is.

Let's say you're afraid to go the dentist. What are you afraid of—the pain? A dentist can numb your teeth and gums so that you can't feel a bit of pain. What's the worst that can happen if you don't go to the dentist? You can get some dreadful gum disease and your teeth can all rot and fall out. Don't get me wrong; I don't like physical pain. But why not turn sitting in your dentist's chair into a positive experience by just letting go of your fears? Close your eyes and use it as a complete relaxation time in which you have absolutely no responsibilities.

Fear is negative and the more you focus on your fears the more they will grow. Rhoda has a terrible phobia about earthquakes. She was going to a therapist after the big Northridge earthquake in Los Angeles because she was in a constant state of anxiety. She could talk about nothing but her fear of earthquakes. Then her insurance refused to pay for any more visits and she stopped going to the therapist. Her phobia mysteriously subsided. Why? Because she stopped dwelling on her fear and just went about her life.

Television and magazines heighten our fears about our health. Don't use butter because the fat will clog your arteries. Don't barbecue meat because the charred fat will cause cancer. Don't use aspartame because it causes cancer. Don't talk too much on a cell phone because you'll get brain cancer. Don't eat eggs or chicken because you'll get salmonella poisoning. Don't eat rare hamburgers because you'll get E-coli bacteria.

I thought that I had thought of everything in life that I had to worry about until our insurance agent called us the other day and said, "Do you want to take out flood insurance?"

"Why?" I asked.

"El Nino is coming!" he said.

Yikes, yet another thing to worry about! How can you be happy when you are constantly living in fear of so many dangers? The answer is to make your personal happiness a priority. Take steps to protect you and your loved ones from the hazards that you can prevent and accept that there are many threats to your safety and health that you just *can't* control. If you can't control a threat, then you need to do whatever you can do to keep it from affecting your happiness.

Fear of Dying

Most of us fear the process of dying and the finality of death. Rosemary confessed to Fran, "I'm so afraid of dying."

"Yes, me too," Fran said, "I'm afraid of all the pain I will have to endure," remembering how her mother had suffered as she was dying from cancer.

"Oh, I'm not afraid of the pain, I'm just so fearful of the finality, the nothingness," Rosemary replied.

I realized that they were afraid of two different things—that how you view your life is directly related to your perception of death. A negative outlook on life usually goes along with a negative outlook on death.

Some people believe in reincarnation—that our souls come back over and over again until we learn what we need to learn. If believing in reincarnation makes you feel more positive towards death, no harm in believing it.

If you *choose* to be happy, you cannot fear death. Thus, you must convince yourself that death is just that really good night's sleep you've always wanted. Why not look forward to not having to have any pressures or responsibilities anymore? By looking at death as the ultimate blessing in disguise, you can conquer your fear of death.

Happiness and fear are not compatible. If you *choose* to be happy you must choose to let go of your fears, phobias and obsessions. Take whatever reasonable precautions you must in order to ensure your safety, and move on. Your inevitable death will come whether or not you spend your life thinking about it. So, if you want to enjoy your life, do what you can to stay healthy and safe and then relinquish your fate over to your Higher Spirit.

Remember, what you focus on is usually what you get. If you focus on your fears, they will come true. If you focus on enjoying your life and being happy, that will come true.

Fear of Success

Many people satisfy their own self-fulfilling prophecies of failure by thinking such self-defeating thoughts as, "If I succeed I'll have to keep up a fast pace and I'll get sick." Or, "If I succeed I'll have to keep succeeding or else I'll feel like a failure." This way of thinking ensures that you will never be happy.

Fear of Failure

Are you afraid to try something new because you fear that if you try and fail, you will be embarrassed? "I will have wasted my time," you say. Or, "I will have wasted my money." "Everyone will think I'm a loser." You fear the embarrassment of failure, so you never try anything. Then you are unhappy. True, if you don't try anything you will never fail. Of course, you will never succeed either.

It is far better to have tried and failed than to never have tried at all. If you don't try, you will never know whether you could have achieved your dream or not.

Fear of Rejection

Most people fear rejection at one time or another. They fear walking into a party alone and having no one talk to them. They fear going on a job interview and being told that they aren't qualified. They fear going on a blind date and having the other person not like them.

Do you fear not being pretty or handsome enough? Not smart enough? Not educated enough? Not interesting enough? Remember, you can't please all of the people all of the time. If you *choose* to be happy, remind yourself that there are plenty of people out there who think that you are smart, good looking, charming and intelligent.

Everyone will think more of you if you think more of yourself. Most people are kind and accepting if you allow them to be. If you exude "happiness vibes" you will be accepted easier than if you give out sad vibes. Happy people have more friends than unhappy people. By taking control of your life and *choosing* to be happy, you will feel more confident and will not fear rejection. If others are foolish enough to reject you, you should have compassion for them, as they have lost the benefit of your company.

Fear of Relationships

Relationships don't have to be hard work. If a relationship is meant to be, it flows easily. There might be an occasional argument or a major fight, but both you and your significant other possess compatible communication skills that enable you to talk things out. Developing good relationships is the subject for another whole book.

Fear of Intimacy

If you fear intimacy you fear revealing your true self to another. This is because you probably fear revealing the real you who has bad thoughts that live deep beneath your smile and flowery words. But you will no longer fear intimacy if you have nothing to hide. In order to conquer your fear of intimacy you must first *choose* to be happy and reprogram your inner thoughts to be more positive, loving thoughts.

Fear of Responsibility

If you fear responsibility it is because you have not accepted becoming an adult. You feel safer having someone else control your life. That way, if you fail, it is his fault, not yours. You will automatically lose your fear of responsibility once you decide to take control of your own life.

Fear of Commitment

Your inability to commit to another person or a cause comes from your lack of confidence in your own decision-making processes. You have not taken control over your life yet if you cannot commit to someone or something you believe in. And if you do not have control over your life, you cannot be happy. Once you *choose* to be happy and have taken control of your life, you will automatically be able to make commitments to others.

Fear of Growing Old

We all fear growing old. It means the loss of our youthful beauty, our good health and our ability to take care of ourselves. Because the odds of becoming ill are greater as we age, we fear getting sick; we fear the pain; we fear not being able to do the things we used to do; we fear that our friends will get sick and die; we fear losing our dignity; and we fear ending up alone.

Overcome your fear of aging by taking control of your life. You fear that which you have no control over. But you *can* have control over your body. How you take care of your body now is directly correlated to the quality of life you will have as you age. If you remain in good health, you can look forward to enjoying all the things that you wanted to do in your "golden years." Perhaps it was traveling, or finally writing that novel, or taking up oil painting.

Your happiness is also contingent on your attitude towards aging. If you see old age as something to dread, it will become dreadful. If you see old age as a time to reap the rewards of a life well-lived, you will reap the rewards. You can be a shiny old Rolls Royce or a beat up old Toyota. *It's your choice.*

Fear of Being Alone

Loneliness is a self-inflicted torture. It is more than just being alone in this world. It is your innermost thoughts separating and alienating you from the rest of society. In order to not feel lonely, you must form a

connection to other people through your work and other act
need to form bonds with other people who have similar interests and
ways of thinking. By consciously taking action to form these connec-
tions and friendships you are taking control of your own life.

Fear of Poverty

Poverty only happens to victims. You will never be a victim as long
as you *choose* to take control of your own life. In order to overcome
your fear of poverty you need to plan for your financial future. This
means making the sacrifices you need to make in the here and now,
but does not mean you need to deny yourself everything you want. It
means spending in moderation and controlling your urges for immediate gratification. Take control of your financial future by learning all
that you need to know about investing your money safely and wisely.
Again, this is the subject of another whole book.

Fear of Abandonment

Taking hold of the reins of your life doesn't mean that you don't
need other people, but it does mean that should something happen to
your mate, children, coworkers or friends, that you have enough control over your life to establish new support groups. If you are secure
and confident in your ability to take care of yourself, you will never
fear being abandoned by anyone.

Chapter 6

Forgive

If you are from Planet Earth probably one or more people in your life have hurt or disappointed you in some way. This could be a parent, child, friend, lover, spouse, coworker or total stranger. But the person you are mad at is probably going about his life completely oblivious to your pain and anger. He really isn't even thinking about what he did or didn't do to you. Odds are he isn't even feeling one little pang of guilt or remorse. The only person who is being affected by your pain and anger is *you*. Anger creates high blood pressure, headaches, stomachaches, ulcers and other diseases, some very painful, some terminal. If you are walking around harboring ill feelings for anyone, you are only hurting yourself.

Let go of your vindictive thoughts. Forgive the person who may have hurt you. Try to put yourself in his shoes and think of all the possible scenarios as to why he did what he did to you. Remember that he is only a product of his genetics and environment. Give him every excuse in the world. But forgive him so that you can be happy. This doesn't mean that you have to be his best friend, it just means you have forgiven him for what he has or hasn't done and that you have made a decision to let go of your anger and go on with your life.

> ❧ *Forgiving yourself and others for past mistakes and hurts relieves the pain in your soul and opens up your heart for love and happiness.* ❧

To hold a grudge means that you are maintaining an intense connection with a person with whom you might not have wanted to have a relationship with in the first place.

If you *choose* to be happy, find methods to get rid of your anger. It can be meditation, yoga, kick boxing, listening to music, or anything that works for you. The best emotional outlet for anger is talking things out. I always know that when I'm angry with someone I can call my husband and talk it through with him. Just the act of sharing the story of your anger and having someone validate your irritation releases the pressure of the rage. If you haven't got a mate, a best friend or family member that you can call to release your fury, just writing down your angry feelings will make you feel better.

Think Before You React

Just because someone cuts you off in traffic or makes a U-turn in front of you and almost causes a flammable truck to veer into you doesn't make that driver a bad person. Perhaps this is a very good person who just happens to be a bad driver. Try to talk yourself out of your anger.

Let's say that today is the day you've finally decided that you're going to be happy. You want to be a nice person and so you let someone cut in front of you in traffic, but that person does not wave and say thank you. Now, you decide that it doesn't pay to be nice and you are not happy anymore because your kindness didn't work one time in this particular circumstance. Perhaps that person just found out that something awful just happened to his wife and he's rushing home to her. Or worse, perhaps that person didn't have any arms with which to wave. And even if that person had no reason not to wave and say thank you, perhaps that person is unhappy. Have compassion and give everyone the benefit of the doubt.

Kenny is a perfect example of inner anger that unleashes itself when he gets behind a steering wheel. One day we were in the parking lot of a market and the woman in front of him was waiting for someone to pull out of a parking space. It was taking a long time and there was a line of cars honking at us to move. Kenny leaned on the horn. The woman wanted the parking space and wouldn't move. Kenny screamed and yelled. Finally, he got out of the car and banged on her window and started screaming at her to move. When he came back to the car his face was red with anger.

I said, "That's why you have high blood pressure, you always get so angry at insignificant things."

He replied, "What? Me angry? I was just expressing myself."

People who get angry all the time don't even realize that they are getting angry.

How would you react to the same situation? The woman in front of you in the market parking lot is waiting for someone to pull out so she can get the exact space she desires even though there are 20 other spaces available. A more effective way of dealing with the same situation would be:

A) Lean on the horn.

B) Scream out the window.

C) Go around the woman.

D) Wait patiently.

E) Ram your car into hers.

A happy, positive person will choose "C" as his first choice and "D" as his second choice. After all, timing is everything in life. Let's say an armored car is pulling up to the market entrance and there is going to be an armed holdup. It is possible that if you parked your car and got to the market entrance three minutes earlier you could have been taken hostage or even shot by robbers in ski masks. So, you are actually *lucky* because this woman may have saved your life.

If you *choose* to be happy, let go of your anger. Stop getting mad. Stop blaming people. Stop thinking everyone is stupid. Realize that everyone is doing the best he or she can. Some people aren't as smart as you. Some people aren't as highly evolved intellectually or emotionally as you. Some people aren't aware enough to control their anger. Realize that it is their problem, not yours. Let it go.

Anger turns into hostility. Hostility is a "stuck" emotion. Hostile people are cynical and mistrusting. If you are cynical and mistrusting, you cannot possibly be happy.

Forgive Your Parents

I have several friends in their mid-forties who are still angry with their parents and blame everything that is wrong with their lives on them.

Nancy is 42 years old and still gets tears in her eyes when she speaks of how her father abused her physically when she was a child. She is deeply troubled because she doesn't understand what she did to deserve this abuse. She tries so hard to please her father. In the back of her mind she still believes he hurt her because she wasn't good enough. She is only hurting herself more by not letting go of this past hurt.

Nancy wants her father to see the error of his ways. She wrote him a letter letting him know how much he hurt her. He never answered the letter. She confronted him. Of course, he denied any wrongdoing. She has confronted her mother, a loyal wife who defends Nancy's father. Nancy has tried to get her father into therapy with her, but he is resistant to outside help. It is highly unlikely that Nancy's father will ever admit that he hurt her or apologize for something that in his mind he doesn't think he did.

Nancy believes that if her father gives her a logical reason why he treated her so badly and apologizes that she will be able to forgive him and her pain will disappear. Then she will be happy.

But Nancy is beating her head against a wall. She is dealing with a 70-year-old man who refuses to accept that he could have done something wrong. If Nancy *chooses* to be happy she must let go of this issue and forgive him even if there is no excuse for his behavior. This does not mean that she should condone his behavior. It only means she should forgive him, let go of past injustices, and be happy.

Lynette drinks too much alcohol, has an eating disorder, shops compulsively, and is a perfectionist. She has had multiple marriages and divorces. Now she is a middle-aged woman searching desperately for a man to take care of her. She blames the fact that her life is so screwed up on her mother, who has a controlling, judgmental personality. Lynette needs to stop using her mother as an excuse for her problems.

Angela blames her addiction to methamphetamines on her father's divorce from his second wife, whom she had considered her "mother" for 18 years. "How else was I supposed to get through my dad's divorce!" she screams, in defense of taking drugs. It is clear that she is blaming her controlling father for her drug habit because of her inability to take control of her own life.

To use your "abusive" childhood or your "dysfunctional" family as an excuse for your inability to control one or more aspects of your life is to pass the blame because you don't want to accept responsibility for your own behavior. Let's face it, everyone's family is pretty much dysfunctional.

> ❧ *If you can't let go of your childhood*
> *you can never become an adult.*
> *And if you can't become a functioning adult,*
> *you can never be happy.* ❧

If you *choose* to be happy, stop blaming your parents for your problems and take responsibility for your own behavior. Let go of the past and forgive those who have hurt you. And, if you are to forgive others and tolerate their humanness, then you must forgive yourself and tolerate your own humanness.

Forgive Your Own Flaws

If you insist on being perfect you will always be unhappy because nothing in life is perfect, even you.

If you are a perfectionist you are paralyzed by what might happen if you don't make the perfect decision. You think that if you can't do something perfectly, you might as well not do it at all. You feel inferior if you don't do a task perfectly. You just won't do something unless the situation is perfect. You won't put on a bathing suit until you lose 15 pounds so you refuse to go on that cruise. Then you stay home and eat because you're upset you didn't go on the cruise and, of course, gain another 15 pounds. Then you are even more disgusted with your imperfections than before.

Most likely you want to be perfect to impress others because you think that you are more imperfect than other people. The irony is that a lot of people are intimidated rather than impressed by people who appear to be too perfect. Most people will respond to you more positively when you appear less perfect and more vulnerable. It makes them feel better about their own imperfections.

Ana is a perfectionist. She spends endless hours organizing her notes into files and getting ready to start some business, which, of course, she never starts. She files every little newspaper and magazine clipping that might come in handy in the next 50 years. She is so absorbed in organizing her environment that she never really accomplishes anything. When you tell her this, she insists she's going to get it together once she gets the boxes in the garage reorganized (for the 40th time.)

Strive for personal growth and achievement, not perfection. If you *choose* to be happy, accept that no one or nothing in life is perfect—not even you.

Let Go of the Thought "I'll be Happy When…"

It is human nature to aspire to have something you don't have, to be with someone you aren't with, or to achieve something you haven't achieved. Sometimes these dreams motivate you to do things that bring you great success and fulfillment. But often these dreams bring you great disappointment and misery.

"I'll be happy when I meet Mr. Perfect." Then you meet and marry him. All of a sudden, Prince Charming goes bald, grows a potbelly, develops a chronic gas problem and loses his job.

"I'll be happy when I meet my dream woman." You wine her and dine her, buy her presents, charm her. She finally agrees to marry you. Ten years later you can't figure out why you are married to this aging nag with cellulite rippling her thighs and a head full of hair rollers. You'll be happy, if only you could get a divorce and marry someone younger and prettier.

You want that dream house. You buy that dream house. Five years later you can't imagine why you were stupid enough to buy a house that has old rusty pipes that are constantly bursting and a roof that leaks— not to mention the exorbitant mortgage payments that are keeping you up all night.

You want a baby. They're so cute and all your friends are having babies. A few years later you're sitting on the laundry room floor buried in vomit-stained bibs while your two toddlers are sprinkling flour on your freshly-washed kitchen floor.

You want that great job—travel, intrigue, a big raise. One year later the boss is a slave driver and you just can't get on one more airplane.

You want that shiny new BMW and finally buy it. After the novelty has worn off, you discover it is a gas guzzler and overheats all the time, not to mention that the repair bills are eating up all of your paychecks.

❧ Happiness is a state of mind, not an acquisition. ❧

Remember, all that glitters is not gold. You are setting yourself up for grave disappointment if you think that any person, possession or achievement can bring you true happiness. Once you have accepted this truth, you will be free to work on the mindset that will bring you true happiness and inner peace.

Triumph Over Your Addictions

You know that you are dealing with an addiction if you feel tense when you do not have that substance. If you are always thinking about that next cigarette, that next drink, that next piece of chocolate cake, that next dose of heroine, that next anything—you are addicted.

Sometimes even good habits become addictions. We try to be too good, too perfect. We diet and exercise to extremes because we want to be admired and accepted for our beauty by our peers so we become anorexics or bulimics. If your habit is hurting your body and you can't stop doing it, your good habit has become an addiction.

If you refuse to let go of your self-destructive behavior you are daring the devil. If you still smoke, you are saying that the quality of your life is not as important as your immediate gratification. You do know that it is only a matter of time before you will get one or more smoking-related illnesses. If you eat too much, your behavior says that how you feel about how you look and how healthy you are is less important than the immediate gratification of eating that bag of potato chips.

Negative physical behavior, such as smoking, alcohol abuse, over-eating, under-eating, or any type of substance abuse is addictive behavior that is sabotaging your happiness. You cannot like yourself if you know you are putting substances in your body that will ultimately hurt it and cause you pain.

In order triumph over your addictions you must stop thinking of yourself as an addictive personality because it is a negative self-fulfilling prophecy.

❧ The mother of all addictions is the addiction
to unhappiness and self-destruction. ❧

.If you want to stop any addiction, the first step is to finally decide that you deserve happiness. Forgive yourself when you relapse. Get right back up and start again. The trick to breaking any addiction is to never give up. You will never be happy unless you have control over your body.

Chapter 7

Snap Out of Your Depression

When someone asks "How are you?" do you automatically whine "I'm so depressed." Just labeling yourself a depressed person is enough to make you fall into the deep dark hole of despair. If you *choose* to be happy, you must *choose* to see yourself as a person who rarely gets depressed.

Depression is a sense of hopelessness. You feel that your life is not worth living. That life is too hard. You feel that you have no control over your life. No matter how hard you have tried, you have been beaten down. You feel that your life is a failure and that you have no reason to live. This emotional state of mind causes you to feel overwhelmingly tired and lethargic.

Depression is a "stuck" emotion. It becomes a way of dealing with the world. When you are depressed, you don't feel sad, but rather indifferent and apathetic. You develop a negative sense of yourself and feel worthless, guilty and helpless—but sometimes a depression can become a catalyst for a positive life-changing action. Diane Ackerman writes in *Parade Magazine* (January 1997) *The Fears that Save Us* that "Just as physical pain warns us of potential damage to the body, emotional pain help us avoid more complicated threats to life and limb." Depression is a warning sign that something about our lives is making us unhappy and we need to do something about it.

She writes that "Our negative behavior evolved at a time when humans lived in small bands of hunter-gatherers. Anxiety played a role in our ancestors' lives by alerting them to potential threats so that they could devise a lifesaving response. We still act like hunter-gatherers, but our anxiety doesn't sift what is important from our more civilized world. Worry kicks in even when we don't need it, want it, or know how to stop it. We keep checking to make sure that we won't be abandoned, won't be sacrificed if wild animals attack or won't be left to starve. Faced with adversity or anxiety, many of us become depressed."

"Depression also elicits concern and nurturing. Other people tend to make allowances for the depressed person who may ignore the normal schedules or obligations of society. 'I'm the helpless child,' the depressed person implies. 'Protect me, embrace me, and tell the world I'm not available for awhile.'"

One of the reasons it is so difficult to snap out of a depression is that when you are depressed all you usually feel like doing is sleeping or just moping around. It is almost impossible to pull yourself out of a depression if you give in to your lethargy for any length of time.

Sometimes one discouraging event can trigger a feeling of despair. Often, it is our level of hormones—estrogen for women, testosterone for men—that create these mood swings. When you are feeling hopeless you can only see what is wrong with your life and you are blind to what is right with your life. There is a black cloud hanging over your head and you are too tired to do anything about it.

Other times you are feeling happy but your mate, children or someone close to you is depressed and you "catch" their depression as if it was the chickenpox. If you are living with someone who is depressed, you have three choices: You can allow him to pull you down into the deep, dark abyss with him; you can ignore him and go about your business; or you can try to pull him up to your level of happiness. If you have tried to pull someone close to you out of a depression and all that happens is that the dark cloud moves over your head, you are allowing that person to make you unhappy. Remember, *no one* has a right to make you unhappy.

When you are depressed, no one wants to be with you, which, of course, leads to further depression because you get even lonelier. Most people would rather have root canal than spend the day with you when you are miserable. If you give in to the black cloud it gets bigger and bigger. If you *choose* to be happy, you must fight the black cloud and replace it with sunshine.

Give Yourself 24 Hours

Allow yourself a full day in which to wallow in the misery of your depression and feel sorry for yourself. The catch is that after 24 hours you are no longer allowed to be depressed. This doesn't necessarily mean that whatever was making you depressed has disappeared. It only means that you have rested enough and have given up enough of your life over to your depression.

Find the Root of Your pain

Your depression might be triggered by a specific situation, event, person, or any combination of the above such as the loss of a loved one, divorce, moving, loss of a job and so forth.

If you can't pinpoint the exact reason for your depression, you should consult a psychiatrist who can determine whether your depression is chemical and/or hormonal and will respond to one of the many new drugs on the market. Chemical depression can be genetic. Your doctor can give you tests to find out if your depression is biological and then prescribe the appropriate medication.

However, if you are depressed and know exactly what is depressing you, your depression is probably not chemical or hormonal and will not respond to medication. You are depressed in reaction to a particular event or situation.

Try to figure out what it is you need to do to stop the pain. Sometimes the whole tooth is rotten and has to be pulled out. Other times the problem can be fixed as easily as filling a cavity. You must identify the source of the pain in order to relieve the pain.

Refuse to Give in to Your Depression

Giving in to your depression is like giving in to a terrorist. If you allow the terrorist within you (your depression) to keep on sabotaging your happiness, you will never win the fight.

Write it Down

The most effective way to get through a depression is to think it through on paper. It doesn't matter how well you write or spell. All that matters is that you are able to express your thoughts, pains and fears in a way that you will be able to read again in 24 hours. By doing this you will be able to better understand what you were feeling or are still feeling. This will help you identify the root of your pain.

Take Action

It is the frustration and lack of control over an event or person in our lives that makes us depressed. When some event or person triggers one of your depressions you can react by giving in to it and climbing under the covers or by taking a positive action. Taking a positive action will give you a sense of control over the situation.

Move On

In return for granting yourself the luxury of hiding under the covers for a day, you must promise yourself that when you wake up you will fight your depression with every ounce of energy you can muster up. You will literally force yourself to make phone calls and sound happy and energetic. You will force yourself to get dressed and go out and be with other people. You will do anything positive that takes your mind off of your unhappiness.

Solve Each Problem

It's like handling paperwork. Efficiency experts say that the fewer times you actually touch paperwork the quicker you can get your work done. For instance, when opening mail, open each letter and respond to it immediately, then file it appropriately.

In the same way, take each problem that is causing your depression, handle it, and then file it. Some of the problems will reappear. Each time a problem reappears, handle it to the best of your ability and then file it away again. Never let problems pile up on top of each other because they will become too overwhelming.

Release Your Depression

Once you have done everything you can do to solve whatever problem or problems have made you depressed, let them go as if you were releasing white doves into the sky. Harping on what caused your depression will only make you more depressed. Once you have a sense of control over what was making you depressed, your depression will subside.

Exercise

Your body is an incredible piece of machinery that must be kept fine-tuned to operate at its optimum. Exercise decreases your blood cholesterol and lowers your high blood pressure. It reduces the risk of heart attacks and strokes. It lowers the risk of colon cancer, helps speed digestion, helps your lungs function more efficiently, and can help control diabetes by lowering blood sugar levels. Regular exercise is good for the central nervous system and helps improve brain function. It reduces stress, curbs appetite, and helps you to think more clearly. Exercise also increases self-esteem. If you are in top physical condition, you look better and thus feel better about the way you see yourself. Exercise releases your endorphins, which are the natural pain killing hormones in your body that make you feel euphoric.

In a study done at Concordia University in Montreal over six weeks, 86 women completed mood surveys before and after exercise. Exercising put women in a much better humor, especially those whose spirits were the lowest before they started working out.

Socialize

Get out of your house! Positive interaction with other people will help you fight off your depression. Sometimes just taking an upbeat action, like forcing yourself to sign up for a class that you've been wanting to take or making a phone call about a job you are interested in is all it takes to lift the black cloud.

Don't Force Anyone or Anything

Good things happen easily and naturally. If you must work too hard or force something to happen, then it wasn't meant to happen. If you relax with whatever you are trying to achieve and if it is something that is meant to be, you will notice how easily information you need and people who can help you flow into your life.

Sometimes I will be writing something and that night I will be reading a magazine or newspaper and the exact information I need will just pop out at me. For instance, the other day I was frustrated trying to communicate with my father-in-law because his hearing aids weren't working well enough anymore. The next day I was at the health club and got into a casual conversation with a woman and just happened to ask what she did for a living. She said she was an audiologist. I told her about my problem with my father-in-law's hearing aids. She told me about an inexpensive device he could use that was far superior to his hearing aids. She got me a sample set. The results were amazing. Life had somehow brought me exactly what I needed. All I had to do was put myself out there and be friendly.

Don't Rush Anyone or Anything

Everything happens in its own good time. Relax and just do the things you enjoy. Stop trying to make everyone you meet into your prospective soul mate. Trust that the right person will come along once you have found your own happiness. Stop making every opportunity into "the opportunity of your life" and realize that opportunities always abound for happy people.

When you stop focusing on potential results and focus on the process, you will finally start enjoying your life. And once you start enjoying your life, you will give out the happy energy that attracts the kind of mate and career opportunities that you want.

> ❧ *If you want to attract happiness,*
> *you've got to project happiness.* ❧

Chapter 8

Magic Formulas for Joy

Are you convinced everything will turn out badly? Are you always **saying** "With my luck . . . "? Even if you put on a smile and act positive, are your innermost thoughts negative? Does your negativity taint everything you do? Then, you have a disease I call "chronic negativity." If you *choose* to be happy, you must reverse your uncontrollable impulses to be negative. Here's how:

Ignore the Negative

Negative emotions sap your energy and make you feel bad. Negative attitudes are magnets that attract negative events and people. If you *choose* to be happy, refuse to harp on the negative events in your life. Stop rehashing them over and over again—just handle them as quickly as possible and let them go. Train yourself to focus on more positive thoughts and activities and you will automatically feel totally energized.

As you already know, Elizabeth has taught me a lot about happiness. Recently we shared our first childhood memories. The earliest memory she could remember was that she was throwing a tantrum because her mother was on the telephone and wasn't paying attention to her. Her mother slapped her and put her in her room until she stopped crying. A genetically unhappy child would have grown up remembering this as having being a victim of physical abuse. Her mother eventually let her out of her room, but made another phone call. Elizabeth had learned not to throw a tantrum again. She recalls this as a very positive learning experience.

In contrast, my first memory is of being in a crib, crying and screaming for my mother, who I could see out the window outside talking to a neighbor. I remember that she was completely ignoring my needs. I felt neglected and ignored and interpreted this as a negative experience.

*❧ The events in your life are only negative
if you choose to interpret them that way. ❧*

The other night we went to dinner with Elizabeth and her husband. When we got back to Elizabeth and Sam's house—we were staying there—my husband discovered that he must have dropped his money clip containing $400 cash at the restaurant.

Elizabeth said, "Why don't you call the restaurant and ask them if they found it?"

"Don't be ridiculous. There's no way someone's going to find $400 cash and give it back," I said automatically, my negativity forcing itself back into my life.

"Oh, I'm sure if they find it they'll give it back," said Elizabeth with her usual positive attitude.

I immediately called the restaurant to see if anyone had found the money. No one had, but I often wonder if I had been more positive and actually thought that the person who found the $400 cash was going to give it back, would we have gotten it back? Of course, I'll never know.

The point is that I have a tendency to interpret events negatively and Elizabeth has a tendency to interpret events positively. How we perceive life and how we interpret the events in our lives begins at the moment we are born and is about 50% genetic. However, different environmental factors as we are growing up might shape and mold those beliefs even more. This is why two children from the same family can turn out to be so different. One can turn out to be a happy, successful person and the other can turn out to be a criminal.

No one gets through life without problems. Life is, by nature, one problem after another—some big, some small. It's how we perceive our problems and handle them that can make the difference in how much stress our problems create.

Elizabeth has led a blessed life. Very few bad things have ever happened to her. She is married to a wonderful man who treats her like a princess. She has never had financial worries or even had to work. She doesn't have to worry about their lifestyle in retirement. Her children are both terrific. She has a wonderful relationship with her sister. She has a million friends. Everyone loves to be around her because she has such an "up" personality.

However, Elizabeth is now getting what I call her "obligatory 15% life's crises," the challenging life events that we are all bound to have sooner or later if we live long enough. About five or six years ago, her husband, Sam, was diagnosed with cancer.

When I spoke with Sam right after his doctor's appointment, he told me that he had lymphoma of the spleen. His voice was cheerful and happy, not like a person who had just heard he had cancer. He proceeded to tell me that he was very lucky because the doctor had told him that if there was any kind of cancer he was going to get, this was the best kind because it progressed slowly. There was actually excitement in his voice when he told me that the doctor had told him that researchers were on the verge of a cure for a similar disease and that there was great hope that the same cure would work on him.

However, since then, Sam also has been displaying some other very strange and progressive symptoms. He walks with a slow shuffle and holds his body stiff. His personality has changed and he is no longer as enthusiastic about life as he used to be. He has mental confusion and memory loss.

Elizabeth took Sam to a neurologist. She and Sam called me within an hour after they had gotten the diagnosis from the doctor. Elizabeth told me they had good news—that the diagnosis was Parkinson's disease. Good news, I thought. Parkinson's is a degenerative disease of the nervous system that creates changes in one's motor ability as well as mental confusion and memory loss. However, the doctor had told them that the medication he was going to give Sam was going to help some of the symptoms and even reverse other of the symptoms. When Sam got on the phone I tried not to let my negativity show through. I said, "I'm so glad it's good news."

Sam replied, "Good news? It's excellent news!"

Both Elizabeth and Sam are genetically happy people who refuse to dwell on negatives. Happy people will find a way to turn negative events into happy, positive events.

Four days later, Elizabeth and Sam called to tell me the even better news. Sam was really responding well to the medication. After only four pills his personality was changing back into the old, enthusiastic Sam we used to know and once again he was walking with a spring in his step. I truly believe that if they hadn't both been such positive people, the medication would not have worked that well.

They have gone on to enjoy life to the fullest and see their glass as half full. They *choose* to be happy in spite of the cancer and Parkinson's disease and decided that the quality of their lives in the present was most important. They planned vacations, parties and dinner dates and refused to be unhappy about his illnesses.

It doesn't take a rocket scientist to figure out that if you put out positive energy that you get positive results. Elizabeth convinced me through her actions that you could make your own happiness no matter what bad happens to you. And, unfortunately, in reverse, you can make your own unhappiness no matter what good happens to you.

In contrast, Rhoda is chronically negative. During a recent lunch date she confided in me about a friend of hers that she felt was getting a little too close to her. "Emily is so negative. All she does is complain and criticize everyone and everything," Rhoda told me. She went on to tell me that she realized that spending so much time with Emily was making *her* negative and critical of everyone and everything. "I'm going to try very hard not to be as negative and critical as Emily," said Rhoda.

The food came. Rhoda complained that it was "too hot" or "too cold" or "too bland" or the waiter was not attentive enough. She could see her behavior intellectually but she couldn't see it as she was doing it. Rhoda is genetically unhappy. Her mother was a miserable woman who had spent her entire life sitting home, watching television, saving money, doing nothing. But Rhoda, who could see how miserable her mother's life had been, was unable to break through the family pattern.

Most of us are able to see our shortcomings intellectually, but few of us are able to break away from a lifetime of negative thoughts and habits.

Focus Only on the Positive

Whenever you encounter problems, deal with them as quickly and efficiently as possible and then try to focus on the more positive aspects of your day. If you have some work to do that you aren't looking forward to, try making it fun. For example, doing laundry is usually not a joy. However, if you make folding the towels perfectly into a game and make sniffing the fluffy, clean towels into a sensuous experience, it becomes pleasurable.

Studies show that optimists live longer than pessimists because they take better care of themselves rather than slip into bad habits that age them prematurely. "When we express positive emotions, we boost some immunological functions," says John Fahey, M.D., an immunologist at the University of California at Los Angeles. "With negative emotions, immunological functions drop."

Turn Negative Events into Learning Experiences

If you *choose* to be happy, choose to believe that bad things happen to you in order to show you how to achieve good things. For example, if you are single and keep on going on one date from hell after another, you are still in the learning process. After all, how are you going to recognize the right mate for you unless you have experienced the wrong mates? Perhaps your expectations are too high. Possibly you are negating potential mates because you are really frightened of making a commitment to one person. Maybe you are meeting people in the wrong places or your standards are too high. Conceivably you are overestimating your own attributes and there are things about yourself that you need to change. Or maybe you are just dating people who are wrong for you.

Always ask yourself, "What have I learned from this experience?" If it was a successful encounter, figure out what it was that you did that worked. If it was a negative encounter, ask yourself what it was that didn't work.

Adjust Your Attitude

A positive attitude will make you happy. A negative attitude will make you unhappy. Therefore, if you *choose* to be happy you automatically choose to have a positive attitude.

Let's say you always start out with a positive attitude but then you do everything you're supposed to do and you always end up getting disappointed. How do you keep on having a positive attitude when nothing ever works out right for you? Because you *have to* if you *choose* to be happy. If you lose your positive attitude, you lose your drive and motivation, and if you lose your drive and enthusiasm, you will end up unhappy. If you *choose* to be happy, you *choose* to think positive thoughts no matter what.

I often notice the difference in attitudes of elderly people. There are many senior citizens that seem to be sitting around just waiting around to die. They feel too old for new hopes and dreams. They carry life's disappointments in their faces and on their shoulders. These are the chronically negative.

In contrast, I see Ben, a 102-year-old man who still drives and still works out at the health club every day. Or Billy, a happy 76-year-old man who is always busy thinking about what new business he wants to start or where he wants to go on his next trip.

Become a Realistic Optimist

Sometimes pessimists are just more realistic than optimists. Just being positive all the time won't protect you from life's disappointments.

Don't set yourself up for failure by being unrealistically optimistic. Valerie finds one Mr. Perfect after another. Each time she is positive that this one is her soul mate, but each time she is disappointed.

- View setbacks as temporary. If you tend to think that unpleasant events will last a long time, perhaps even a lifetime, you will feel helpless to change them. Don't explain your misfortunes to yourself with words like "I never" and "I always."

- Don't take everything personally or blame yourself for events you can't control. If you invite someone to come with you to a dinner party and she turns you down, it may just be that she has other plans.

- Don't assume that just because you believe something about yourself, no matter how negative, that it is true.

- When you notice that you are negative and unhappy, ask yourself, "What real reason is there to feel this way?" In most cases, negative thoughts are distortions. Challenge them. Take a good look at people who *really* have it bad. Maybe reach out and do something to help them.

• When something goes wrong, don't harp on it. Focus on why it happened and what you can do to make it better.

• Never preface a sentence with the words "with my luck." By declaring yourself an unlucky person you are creating your own self-fulfilling prophecy and automatically setting yourself up for bad luck.

• Assume the best about everyone. If you find out later on that you were wrong about that person, forgive yourself, extricate him from your life, and move on.

• Assume the best about every situation. Learn to enjoy everything you do by accentuating the positive and de-emphasizing the negative. But don't always take this literally. You should always look at both sides of a situation before making important decisions. Exploring the "What if?" of a situation is not being negative, it is just being realistically cautious.

Negative Thinking May Make You Sick

If you are always unhappy and thinking negative thoughts you are creating negative energy inside your body. Negative thoughts are breeding grounds for both mental and physical disease.

Norman Cousins proved that happiness and laughter arrested, and in some cases cured, some forms of cancer. Think about all the people you know. Isn't it true that the unhappy, negative people seem to get sick all the time while the happy, positive people seem to be hearty and healthy?

Karen Barr, in an article called *The Nocebo Effect* writes: "A patient in a cardiac ward in a Catholic hospital takes a turn for the worse and is about to die. Doctors call a priest to administer last rites. He performs his duty, but mistakenly addresses the not-so-sick patient in the next bed, who dies within 15 minutes." This true story, told originally by Herbert Spiegel, M.D., a New York City psychiatrist, is an example of "The Nocebo Effect" in which negative beliefs, whether expressed by yourself or someone else, can have a frightening impact on your health.

According to Herbert Benson, M.D., an associate professor of medicine at Harvard Medical School, a staggering 60-90% of common medical conditions can be exacerbated by "The Nocebo Effect"—chest pain, headache, asthma—all conditions for which there may not be a specific cause such as a bacteria or virus. These ailments can be influenced by stress, which in turn, may be influenced by our thoughts. Scientists can pinpoint how negative thoughts may contribute to illness, but new research is showing that areas of the brain in which fear is expressed are connected to places in the brain that directly affect key organs such as the heart. So if a person is afraid, they could trigger life-threatening irregular heartbeats. Of course this doesn't mean that if you fear breast cancer you will develop it. Neutralize your fear with facts. "Irrational fear is most harmful," says Dr. Spiegel.

According to studies at the University of Pittsburgh, patients with a pessimistic attitude appeared to be at greater risk of death from cancer. "It may be that having negative expectations about the future can actually end one's life prematurely," say study researchers.

Roberta Pollack Seid, Ph.D. in *Shape* (November 1996) writes, "Scientists have discovered that the immune system and the brain carry on a two-way communication. For instance, research shows that long-term stress—and even short-term stress like preparing for an exam—can weaken the body's defenses."

But Margaret Kemeny, Ph.D., director of the Norman Cousins Program in Psychoneuroimmunology at the University of California, Los Angeles, says "This doesn't mean that people cause their own diseases."

Roberta Pollack Seid, Ph.D. goes on to write, "It's not whether an emotion is 'bad' or 'good,' it's how you react to it that affects your immune system ... people who repress unpleasant emotions have less favorable immune responses than those who accept and deal with them."

Sheldon Cohen, Ph.D., a psychologist at Carnegie Mellon University in Pittsburgh, exposed 276 healthy men and women to a cold virus. Those with long-term stress (lasting longer than a month) were more than twice as likely to succumb to the bug as those who were less stressed. Chronic stress taxes the body's immune system, making it more susceptible to illness.

The physiological response to tense situations and/or a continual assault of milder ones will eventually speed the bruising and hardening of the arteries. Plaque will build up, a clot will spring loose, and then you will get a heart attack. Duke University researchers Redford Williams and John Barefot have shown that people who come across as hostile on standardized questionnaires seem to suffer more heart attacks, earlier, than those who appear to be more easygoing.

Research from James Blumenthal at Duke University suggests that it isn't exactly anger or hostility that puts you at risk, but rather the tendency to experience almost any negative emotion more intensely than most other people. This includes emotions such as fear, disappointment, anxiety or frustration. During stressful situations, high responders are more likely than non-responders to produce excessive levels of fight-or-flight hormones like cortisol and norepinephrine. If every new situation or petty hassle touches off a battlefield response, researchers say, it is only a matter of time before indigestion and insomnia become chronic or your heart strains under the load. Blumenthal states, "It seems that negative emotions more readily put people in danger and the people who experience these emotions most deeply are not necessarily the hostile personalities or the classic Type A's."

Think Healthy

Your body is like a fine-tuned Ferrari. If you don't put top quality fuel in it, it won't run well. If you don't take care of all the moving parts, the engine will go bad. If you don't take it out for a good run regularly, the carburetors will get clogged. If you let it sit in the garage, it will get rusty.

Most people are less healthy and fatter than just a decade ago despite constant media coverage about the obesity epidemic. Alan, a man in his early forties, is the epitome of bad health. He eats greasy foods off a catering truck every day even though he knows that it is making him fat and clogging his arteries. He smokes and drinks too much. Is his willpower so weak that he just can't say no to immediate gratification? Does he have a death wish? Does he have so little self-esteem that the quality of his life doesn't matter?

The answers are "yes, yes and yes." Alan is the classic "enabler." He has a wife who refuses to work and who is always sick. She sits home all day and watches television shopping programs. They never go anywhere because they never have enough money because she buys so much junk. He is the classic "victim." He is passive and does everything everyone tells him to do. It is almost impossible not to take advantage of Alan's good nature. Not taking care of his body is part of this behavior. He is setting up a self-fulfilling prophecy that he will eventually get a dreadful disease that will again *prove* that he is a victim. Being a victim gives him an excuse for not achieving anything with his life. This gives him a reason to be unhappy, which is the role in which he is the most comfortable.

If you *choose* to be happy, then you *choose* to feel good physically. In order to feel good physically you must give up certain bad habits. Turn off the television. Hide that remote control. Hide that chocolate. Throw away that cheeseburger. Go to the gym. If you find excuses why you cannot do this, like "I haven't got time"—*make time*. Give up something else. If you are sabotaging your good health, then you haven't made a decision to be happy and you might as well stop reading this book right now.

Happiness Pills

Most antidepressants such as Prozac have potentially dangerous side effects along with the benefits. Fortunately, there is a middle ground between taking a chemical drug with slight or moderate toxicity and taking nothing.

Small doses of aspirin may help prevent anxiety and depression. Psychologist Mark Ketterer, along with the mental health Science Center in Detroit and the University of Oklahoma, studied the emotional effects of aspirin on 174 male patients who were undergoing diagnostic procedures for coronary artery disease. Nearly 60% of the subjects had been taking a child's dose (80 milligrams) every day or an adult tablet (325 milligrams) every other day to help prevent blood clots. The rest of the men were not taking aspirin. All of the patients were interviewed about their moods. Wives and close friends also provided information about the subjects' behavior.

Those who took aspirin were significantly less depressed, anxious and worried. They also had fewer fights with their spouses and on average fell asleep in 10 minutes—less than half the time it took the others. The study's findings have yet to be confirmed in clinical trials, but Ketterer and his fellow researchers say it comes as no surprise that aspirin may help improve mood.

Fish oil may make you happy, too. National Institutes of Health researchers Joseph R. Hibbein, M.D. and Norman Salen Jr., Ph.D. both think patterns of depression in this country may correlate with aspects of our diet. Our ancestors, who ate less saturated fat and more polyunsaturated fat, specifically omega-three fatty acids which are essential for heart health, also were much less likely to suffer from depression.

Societies that consume large quantities of fish and omega-three fatty acids, such as Japan and Taiwan, report lower depression rates. Hibbein and Salen believe that these fats may be as critical to the healthy functioning of neural membranes as they are to arteries. Their research suggests that mental and physical well-being hinge on the type as well as the amount of fat we eat. And even though the omega-three/depression connection has yet to be verified in the lab, it makes good sense to eat more omega-three-rich foods such as salmon, mackerel, sardines, lake trout, tuna, crab and bass, if only for the heart-healthy benefits.

Turn Negatives into Positives

No one is exempt from disease or accidents. To be human is to be vulnerable. Christopher Reeve was a vital and healthy husband, father and actor. In one split second a horseback riding accident devastated his and his family's life. But instead of letting his total paralysis keep him down, he turned it into a positive. After his paralysis, he still directed movies and worked to get legislation to provide funding in order to find a cure for spinal cord injuries.

Jim Brady, President Reagan's press secretary, was shot at the same time Reagan was shot and suffered irreparable damage to his brain. He is in constant pain, but the very drive that propelled him to become press secretary drove him to overcome his tragic disability. Brady and his wife turned a negative into a positive. The man who shot Reagan and Brady had a history of mental problems and yet was still able to walk into a gun store and walk out with a gun. Because of this debilitating misfortune, Jim Brady and his wife, Sarah, were able to pass the Brady bill, which makes it *almost* impossible for anyone to buy a gun and take it out of the store before a background check is run on that person. (Unfortunately, in the case of the Virginia Tech massacre, Seung-Hui Cho, the killer, was able to buy guns because that state prohibits mental health records from becoming public.)

Annette Funicello, the famous Mouseketeer and movie actress once idolized by millions of children, was stricken with muscular dystrophy in her forties. She also turned a negative into a positive by working on behalf of others who have been stricken with the same disease.

It is the positive attitude that all of these people have shown in the midst of their adversity that is the same quality that helped them achieve the success they enjoy. Each chose to turn his or her personal tragedy into a positive for our society.

Princess Diana died in a senseless accident. As much as we all are saddened by the loss, a new and much more important focus is being made on the causes she supported such as AIDS research and removing the landmines that have maimed so many innocent people in Southeast Asia.

An example of how I learned how to turn a negative into a positive is when I was in the cancer ward for 10 days following my cancer surgery. It was during that time that I realized what wonderful friends I had and how blessed I was to have them in my life. Not only were my best friends there for me, but people I hadn't heard from for many years called to tell me that they were praying for me.

One friend in particular with whom I had had a silly fight and hadn't spoken to for several years called me. I was so touched that she had the grace to call that we ended up renewing our friendship, forgiving each other, and becoming close friends again.

Another friend, a man who had been a friend of my husband for many years, offered to give me his kidney if I needed it. It brings tears to my eyes to this day just thinking about it.

And so, ironically, being diagnosed and fighting cancer was one of the happiest times of my life. I wasn't worried about money, because money had no meaning. I wasn't worried about the future, because I didn't know if I had a future. I wasn't worried about being productive because I was too sick to be productive. All I had to think about was getting better and how wonderful and helpful everyone was to me in my time of need. It definitely renewed my faith in human nature. In this way, I turned a negative experience into a wonderful learning experience about people and life.

I've since found out that I'm not the only one who has experienced this strange happiness while fighting cancer. A friend of ours, a judge, was diagnosed with lymphoma about a year after my cancer. He had to undergo chemotherapy and take Prednisone and lost all his beautiful salt and pepper hair. Do you know what he said? "I've never been happier in my life!"

"Why?" I asked, already knowing the answer.

"I haven't got a worry in the world now. I'm beating this lymphoma and that is the only thing in the world that matters," he said.

Amen.

In order for your life to make sense you must believe that life is a process and that all the pain you endure, all the failures, all the accidents, all the strokes of bad luck, are all learning processes.

> ❧ *If you can learn from each bad experience*
> *and turn it into a positive you have made a*
> *major step in creating your own happiness.* ❧

Chapter 9

Win, Win, Win!

Set Goals

You must have goals in order to be happy. This is your reason or reasons to get up in the morning and do something with your life that matters, something that will better just one person or entire mankind.

Leslie constantly goes to psychics and taro card readers looking for the reasons why she always feels miserable and unhappy. I asked her, "Do you know what it is that will make you happy?"

"No. I haven't got a clue," she replied.

"How can you expect to be happy if you don't know what it is that makes you happy?" I asked.

"Maybe that's what wrong," she said, "I don't have any goals."

"Why don't you sit down tonight and write down all the things that would make you happy?" I asked.

"I wouldn't know where to start," she replied.

"If you don't know the specific things that will make you happy, you will never be happy. It's like leaving on a trip without knowing where you are going. You will never get there," I said to her.

Leslie looked frustrated as we hugged and said goodbye. She promised me she would make a list of her goals, but I suspect she won't. The secret of happiness was too simple—it is just a *choice*. I think she much preferred to remain unhappy because she was comfortable being miserable and really didn't want to exert the energy it took to be happy.

Mel is an unhappy and lethargic 60-year-old man who is counting the days to retirement from his dull, union scale job. His late parents, chronically depressed Irish Catholics, believed that the here and now was meant for suffering and that after they died they would go to heaven and be rewarded for all the suffering they had endured by finally being able to have fun. This is the epitome of living in the future. Mel's lack of enthusiasm and motivation is partly genetic and partly early-childhood conditioning, but he could overcome his past negative conditioning

---

by taking charge of his life and *choosing* to be happy. Of course, he probably won't because he is comfortable being unhappy.

The process of fulfilling your dreams is essential to the achievement of your happiness. If you do not do in life what you have a passion and a talent for, then you will never be happy. Give yourself every opportunity to have the life you have always dreamed about. Follow your dreams.

Of course, all successful people know that not all of their endeavors will be successful. When they reach a dead end they accept their losses graciously and move on to the next project. As long as you keep on dreaming and keep on creating challenges you will never be a failure. It's not whether you win or lose, it's how much you enjoy playing the game of life that will make you happy.

❧ *Success is getting up one more time after you fall.* ❧

It's Okay to Rethink Your Goals

If what you are trying to do is not working there is no shame in redefining your goals. Maybe you are doing something that is not well suited for your skills or personality. Maybe your goals are too lofty. Maybe you really don't have enough talent. Is that so terrible to admit? If you have spent your life honing your skills and still do not have a natural talent, perhaps you are trying to go up the down escalator.

If you can't achieve one goal, try another. If you can't achieve that goal, then try another. You must keep trying. Don't ever give up. The most valuable asset for success is persistence. This doesn't mean that if you can't sing that you should keep on trying out for the choir. I'm sure Barbra Streisand would not have been as successful had she not been blessed with such a beautiful voice. Everyone has some talent. Granted, we are not all gifted actors, but we are all special in some way. Happiness is found in finding your own special talents, however spectacular or mundane they may be. There is nothing wrong with just being the best you that you can be and the sooner you accept this and stop comparing yourself to super-achievers, the sooner you will be happy.

Make your life's work something that you truly love to do and you will always be successful. An obstetrician I know recently told me that he had just helped deliver a baby whose mother he had delivered 25 years ago. He beamed with happiness and said that if he never made another dime being an obstetrician, he would still love doing what he does. He said he loved it so much that he would actually be willing to pay to be able to do the same thing. This is a truly happy, successful man.

Your happiness should never depend on whether or not you achieve your dreams and goals. True success is having tried to do what you truly wanted to do. To believe that you will never be happy until you achieve a certain goal is to put happiness in the future and to base your whole happiness on one particular goal. This is foolhardy. Haven't you noticed how successful people manage to find a new goal to achieve in order to keep them motivated and happy? Actors want to direct. Directors want to produce.

> ❧ *Happiness is the **process** of achieving your goals,*
> *not the achievement of your goals.* ❧

My ex-husband used to say, "Success is what a man is willing to settle for." In rebuttal I say, "If you have to just settle on a life, you are not successful."

Success is having goals, meeting those goals one by one, and setting new goals. Once you have achieved all those goals, you are not successful—you are dead. Success is enjoying the process of living, of achieving, of just being. It is enjoying yourself, your work, your mate, your children, your friends, your environment and your world. Success is also being wise enough to accept that if you still haven't met all of your goals, you can still be happy.

> ❧ *Success is the quality of your journey.* ❧

If, on your deathbed, you can say that you truly enjoyed every moment of your life, then you are successful. If you merely achieved what you wanted to achieve, but you didn't enjoy the process, then you weren't successful. *Money should not be a measure of a person's success. State of mind should be.*

Create a Reason to Be

To be happy you must be enthusiastic about life. That means that you have to get out there and live—try new restaurants, travel, meet new people, take classes, participate in sports, read interesting books, see movies, be a part of life. Never stop learning! The happiest people I know are the people who don't have enough hours in the day to do everything they want to do and learn about everything they want to learn about.

When you are out there in the world, exuberant and enthusiastic, you will find your passion. It doesn't matter whether it's Chinese cooking, oil painting, directing films, or photography. It can be anything positive. Find a passion in life. It has been proven that children who are involved in after-school activities such as playing a musical instrument, dancing, gymnastics, or sports are happier, better-adjusted children. Adults who have passions, hobbies and diversified interests are also happier and more well-adjusted.

Once you have discovered or created your passion, motivation will come naturally and you will automatically create your own goals. What made Shaquille O'Neal so full of enthusiasm for basketball? What makes Stephen Spielberg so full of zest for movie making? The secret of happiness is to find something you do well and love to do. The happiest, most successful people always say, "I can't believe I'm being paid to do what I love doing most!"

Now, of course, there is a reality. The odds of your passion taking you to the professional and financial heights as Shaq or Spielberg are quite low. You might be able to do what you love to do only as a hobby. Or, you might be lucky enough to make a living doing what you love to do.

Let's say you love to write but you must drive a bus for a living. Enjoy your passion for writing whenever you have time. But don't let that ruin the rest of your life. Don't resent driving a bus. Learn to enjoy driving your bus. Get to know your regular passengers. Tell jokes. Laugh. Interact with everyone. Make your work into a game. In order to enjoy your life, you must find joy in *everything* you do.

I think we've all encountered people who love what they are doing even if they are making minimum wage sweeping floors just because they love life and enjoy the people they come in contact with. On the other hand, we've all encountered people who are nasty and unhappy no matter how prestigious their positions and no matter how much money they make.

> ❧ *It is not actually what you do but your **attitude***
> *about what you do that will make the difference*
> *between whether you are happy or unhappy.* ❧

.

Write Down Your Goals

What is it that you want to accomplish by the end of tomorrow? By the end of next week? By the end of next month? By the end of this year? By the end of five years? Ten years? By retirement? By the end of your life? What is it you want to say on your deathbed? Remember—it is not your actual goal, but the quest to achieve your goal that will make you happy.

Make Achieving Your Goals Fun

If you create a challenge for yourself that is greater than your skills, you are most likely going to get frustrated and anxious. But if your skills exceed the challenge, you are likely to get bored. As your skills improve, keep on creating more and more goals to challenge yourself.

Don't constantly fixate on your end goal. Set sub-goals that you can reach. Learn to enjoy improving your skills and techniques. Transform your duties into a form of play.

Be Motivated for Positive Reasons

I used to think that whatever motivated me to achieve my goals was okay as long as it served its purpose to motivate me. However, what I noticed was that when I was motivated for negative reasons, I got negative results.

For instance, I used to be motivated to write a bestselling book or an Oscar-winning screenplay in order to prove my self-worth. I was going to show my mother, who said, "Your sister is the smart one in the family." My motive was proving her wrong. This is a negative motivation. It will bring negative results. It always has. It always will.

However, if you are motivated to prove someone wrong in a loving and non-vengeful way, this is not the same as a negative motivation. In an interview with Brett Butler on CNN, he said that the reason he was so motivated to play baseball again after his diagnosis of cancer and ensuing operations was that he had to "prove to the doctors and his wife that they were all wrong." He created his own motivating challenge in order to be a winner.

Network with People

Opportunity does not come knocking at your door—you've got to make your life happen. If you want people to call you, you've got to make your phones hum. Always connect with winners. Success rubs off on you (as do negativity and failure.) Surround yourself with successful people.

Never Give Up

Life is hard but death is pretty unrewarding. Just because nothing you've done in the past has worked, it doesn't mean the next thing you try isn't going to work. And, if the next thing you try doesn't work, try something else. The law of averages shows that *eventually* you will hit something that *does* work.

After years of being a divorcee, I had just about given up on ever finding a normal man with whom to share my life. When I met my current hubby, I was a skeptic. I couldn't believe he was normal because I had decided that there was something wrong with every man I had dated, therefore there had to be something wrong with him. *I was wrong.* We've been married many years.

After I let my condominium go into foreclosure because I owed more than it was worth, I used to drive down the street and look at these cracker box houses and tell myself I would never even own a tiny house like that. I felt defeated and hopeless. Then my aunt died. I found out that she had money and that I had inherited some of it. With the surprise money I was able to buy us a beautiful townhouse overlooking the Pacific Ocean.

While I was a successful interior designer there was a recession. Very few people were buying houses or redecorating and I couldn't make ends meet. Then I met my partner and together we formed a custom furniture leasing company that was very successful.

The fun of getting up every morning is to see what surprises life has in store for you!

Stop Sabotaging Your Own Life

Most people are their own worst enemies when it comes to happiness. They just don't know how to get out of their own way. They just can't see what it is they are doing to create their own misery.

In order for you to see how you are sabotaging your own happiness you must be willing to be honest about who you are and what you can realistically accomplish. In spite of what many of the famous motivators say, everyone has limitations.

> ~ *Often the degree of our happiness and unhappiness*
> *is based on the amount of space between what*
> *we expect of ourselves and what we actually achieve.* ~

The further we are from achieving what we had hoped to achieve, the unhappier we usually are. If you *choose* to be happy, it might be necessary to accept that perhaps you are not capable of achieving everything you had hoped to achieve. There is nothing wrong with coming to terms with your own limitations. This is not to be confused with failing. This is redefining your goals to make them more within your reach.

Know When to Move On

If you have done everything in your power to make your business successful or to make a relationship or situation work and it is clear that there is nothing else you can do to make it work, maybe it's time to try something else. You are successful because you have taken a situation, given it all you have, recognized defeat, and are ready to move on. Most likely your positive energy will work more successfully in another business or relationship. It is better to go on to the next opportunity than to waste your life enduring something you know will never work. To be successful is to recognize that some situations, businesses and relationships just may not work anymore.

Dick is depressed because his business is in deep financial trouble. He can think of nothing else except how miserable his business is making his life. Yet he clings on to it because he doesn't want to give up. He always argues, "I've put too much money into this business to just walk away." But sometimes it is better to cut your losses and move on. Remember, no one and nothing, including your business or job, has the right to rob you of your inherent right to pursue happiness.

Dick is clinging to a business that is making him miserable because he still believes that he can turn it around. He believes that to quit now would make him a failure. All of the great motivators such as Napoleon Hill and Anthony Robbins tell us that those who "persevere under the greatest adversity" are those who end up winning. He is caught in a tug-of-war with the school of thought that says life is too short to spend one minute doing something you don't enjoy doing and the school of thought that says to be successful you must persevere.

The question is, at what point do you give up what is not working and spend your time more productively doing something that has a better chance of working? Certainly, if a relationship were causing Dick as much grief as his business causes him, he would have walked away from it a long time ago. We all come to forks in the road of life and we must each decide which road to take. Do we quit and take a chance on the unknown or stay and fight? "Better the devil you know than the devil you don't know?" The word "devil" connotes negativity, and if we *choose* to be happy we *choose* to eliminate as much negativity as possible from our lives.

Changing your path does not mean you have failed. It means you are smart enough to realize that something isn't working and have moved on to try something else that may work. You cannot be happy chasing a dream that will never happen.

If you don't enjoy your life as it is now, find a way to change it. Change what you do for a living. Change who you spend your life with. Change what you do with your free time. Change your friends. Change the place you live. If you are stuck with people in your life that can't be traded in for new and better models, like children and relatives, change your attitude towards them.

If you tell yourself that you or your life is a failure, you are choosing to see yourself as a loser and thus creating your own unhappiness.

Don't Beat Yourself Up

Always forgive yourself. If you tried, then you have succeeded in trying. You just didn't get the outcome you wanted.

You are only human. Do the best you can whenever you can. If it doesn't work out, accept it. Don't beat yourself up for making a mistake. Be as caring and compassionate to yourself as you would be to a best friend who you want to make feel better.

Take your mind off temporary setbacks by deciding to try something new and different. It doesn't have to be something as lofty as finding a cure for AIDS. It can be as simple as trying a new recipe for brownies.

Chapter 10

Acceptance

Accept What You Cannot Change

Our world is changing rapidly. Computers and technology have taken over and large corporations are merging and getting bigger and bigger. The Internet has made competition even tougher and the world smaller and more integrated. If you *choose* to be happy, you must accept all these changes graciously and focus on the positives of a rapidly changing world rather than the negatives. Accept these changes with love and compassion in your heart because we all have to share our world and its resources with each other. If you allow yourself to become bitter about our evolving world, you are creating your own unhappiness by allowing situations beyond your control to make you unhappy.

Instead, take control of your life and make the changes you need to make in order to adjust to our ever-changing world. Explore new opportunities. Let go of your resistance because it will make you unhappy and sap you of the energy you need to create new opportunities for yourself.

Say Goodbye to Guilt

Accept blame. If something is your fault, simply apologize for your mistake. Most people will accept your apology graciously and gratefully and admire you for your integrity. Never feel guilty for making mistakes. Guilt is a negative emotion that will make you unhappy.

Are you constantly catering to the needs of others rather than your own needs? The president of your condominium's homeowner's association calls and asks you to organize the yearly party. As it is, you cannot find enough time to cut your toenails. You finally assert yourself and say "no," but you feel guilty. Never allow anyone else to make you feel guilty. If you *choose* to be happy, you *choose* to honor yourself and your precious time.

And don't be a guilt giver. Using guilt to manipulate another person is unkind. Being unkind to others will ultimately make you unhappy.

Stop Blaming Yourself or Others

Are you someone who challenges anyone who bumps into you and says something like "Hey Buddy, watch where you're going!" I am not advocating either meekly accepting blame for everything or blaming everything on others. I am a believer in using diplomacy at all times. It doesn't matter who bumped into whom, if you *choose* to be happy, graciously accept some of the blame (even if you aren't to blame) and then let it go. Life is too short and too precious to spend time on a negative emotion like blame.

If everything you do is wrong and your life is a mess, it probably is your fault. However, if you did the best you could, you shouldn't blame yourself. Don't beat yourself up; just proceed to straighten out your life, change the things you can change and accept the things you cannot change.

Always Being Right Is Wrong

Sometimes, especially in an argument with your mate or a close friend, you are positive that you are right about an issue. However, if *choose* to be happy—and to keep that relationship—you realize that it is really not important who is right. What is *really important* is maintaining your loving relationship with that person.

Conquer Your Inferiority Complex

There is no reason for you to feel inferior. If you feel bad about your appearance, do something about it. If you feel bad about not being educated enough, go back to school. If you feel bad that you are not smart enough, read more—exercise your brain. If you feel bad because you are not popular, reach out and make more friends. Focus on your strong points. If you can't think of anything you excel in—find it! *Everyone* is special in some way.

First, decide to change the things about yourself that you *can* change and *accept* the things about yourself you *cannot* change. Next, always accentuate the positive and de-emphasize the negative. Be a makeup artist with your life. Draw attention away from your flaws by drawing attention to your assets.

Accept that you are not perfect. Have a sense of humor about your shortcomings. Let others know you are only human. It will make them feel more comfortable about themselves and like you even more.

Build Your Self-Esteem

Some people have a more healthy self-esteem than others. Some of it has to do with how we came into this world. Part of it has to do with what happened while we were growing up.

In order to build your own self-esteem you must *accept* yourself, flaws and all. This doesn't mean that you can eat yourself into obesity or not groom yourself. It means doing the best with what nature gave you to work with and *accepting*, even having a sense of humor about, the things that nature didn't give you. *Accept* your limitations. Always strive to do the best with the tools that you were given. However, don't beat yourself up for not having the brains, beauty or talent to do or achieve something that is unachievable for you. You can't be happy unless you feel good about yourself.

Life May Not Seem Fair

"Why do so many bad things happen to a nice person like me?" you ask. *Accept* the fact that life may not always *seem* fair. If life were fair, we'd all be born perfect—beautiful, intelligent, rich, healthy, talented and kind. But most of us are born with flaws and have at least some bad things happen to us. Some of us will get through life with just a few cuts and bruises while others of us will be faced with one tragedy after another.

Tom, a man in his mid-forties, was in a terrible car crash when he was a teenager and has been a paraplegic ever since. He is one of these people who always smiles and is continually happy. He turned his handicap into a positive by using it to successfully fight for legislation that has made all of our cities easier for handicapped people. Now he works at a college where he councils handicapped students.

One intoxicated driver changed Tom's whole life. He could have easily spent his entire life bitter and angry with that drunk who hit him, but instead he decided to let go of his anger and make the best of the life that he still had left. To remain angry with the driver would have been to give the driver the power to keep making Tom's life miserable. You can't undo accidents. You can't change a lot of things. There is no use looking back and saying "What if this or what if that...?" Or, "I should have done this or that...." If you *choose* to be happy, you *choose* to *accept* that what happened can't be changed and decide to enjoy your life in spite of what happened. When misfortune strikes, remember the Alcoholics Anonymous serenity prayer, which is "God grant me the serenity to *accept* the things I cannot change, the courage to change the things I can, and the wisdom to know the difference."

Life Can Be Cruel

There has always been and there will always be war, hate, racism, poverty, crime, suffering and death. There have always been accidents, natural catastrophes, pollution and disease. Most of us are powerless to cure the ills of society in any significant way. Certainly we can't control Mother Nature. In order to be happy we must *choose* not to ignore what is going on around us, but to *change* those conditions we can change and to *accept* those conditions we cannot change. You cannot stop most injustices, so stop making yourself miserable about them.

Security Is a Myth

"I am unhappy because I never feel secure," said a friend of mine who is having financial difficulties.

Every adult yearns to re-experience the feeling of security they felt as a child. How good it felt not to worry about the rent or mortgage or losing your job or your mate cheating on you or getting some dread disease. But as every adult learns sooner or later, feeling security is only a mirage. The only *real* security comes from an inner peace within you.

Emotional Security. Your husband can leave you for your babysitter. Your wife can leave you for her private trainer. Your friends can move away and replace you with new friends. Your parents and grandparents are going to get old and die. Your children aren't necessarily going to take care of you in your old age. So, in order to ensure your own happiness, it's important for you to create a *large* support group. Ideally, it should be a balance of family, friends and coworkers along with a church, synagogue or other type of support system. Feeling that you *belong* will make you happy.

But in the end, true emotional security is really an inner feeling that if any of your support system is taken away from you for any reason, you will not crumble. Your emotional security is your belief that you are capable enough to take care of yourself and to create your own happiness no matter what happens to you or your support system.

Physical Security. There is no such thing as physical security. How do you feel physically secure when Mother Nature makes sure she reminds you almost every day that there is no place you can be safe? If the earthquakes and hurricanes don't get you, then it's the tornadoes, mudslides, fires and floods. If you don't die in a heat wave you'll die in the winter storms or a tsunami.

When we take an airplane we worry about a drunken pilot, a skyjacking, ice on the wings, a fire, a bomb, or being sucked out of the exit doors. When we take a train we worry about terrorists sabotaging the tracks and school buses getting stuck at the crossing. When we ride in a car, we worry about a carload of drunken teenagers having a head on collision with us. If we take a cruise, we have to worry about whether or not we're going to hit an iceberg and sink like the Titanic or whether or not we're going to get some kind of poisoning from the food or the air conditioning vents. We can't even go to the zoo without worrying that some monkey is going to spit on us and infect us with the Ebola virus. If you really want to worry, just think how easy it is for some terrorist to drop poison into our water supply.

We all yearn to feel the safety and security we felt as children, but that was really just naivety; there is really no such thing as total security. Life is a precious gift and can be taken away from us at any moment. Joan Rivers wrote, "That's why today is called the present." Life takes strange twists and turns and no one knows how things will turn out. That's what makes life exciting; like a good book, it's a page-turner.

However, in order to feel as secure as possible, do whatever you can to protect yourself, your family, and your home and then go on living, confident that you have done everything you can do. Whatever happens is beyond your control.

If you *choose* to be happy you are obliged to *accept* the conditions and events you cannot change. It is important to develop an inner security—a sense that no matter what happens, you are strong enough to endure it. A sense of security is not external. It comes from a feeling deep within us. The sooner you *accept* the reality that you will never be safe 100% of the time, the sooner you will relax, enjoy life and *accept* what comes your way.

Financial Security. No matter how much money you make, you will probably find a way to spend more. No matter how much money you save for your retirement, you will always find things that you can't afford. No matter what you invest in, there is always a chance you will lose your money.

The safest investment is a certificate of deposit at the bank, which is insured by our federal government. Unfortunately, there is not enough money in the Federal Reserve to cover all the insured certificates of deposits should our banking system collapse.

The second safest investments are treasury bills and treasury bonds, which, of course, are only as good as the strength of our monetary system.

Then there are municipal bonds, but some local government employee can use our money to buy derivatives and lose it all for us.

We can invest in the stock market or mutual funds which, of course, are risky and often have ups and downs not unlike a roller coaster ride. The market plunges and surges every time there is a terrorist scare.

You can stick your money in a numbered account in a Swiss Bank, but who's to know what is going on across the ocean or if there is turmoil in the country and they can seize your account. Not to mention the possibility that you will get Alzheimer's disease and forget where you wrote down the account number.

You can buy real estate, but a recession could depreciate the value of your property and you could end up with no equity left. Or worse, you could lose your job, not be able to afford the payments and property taxes, and the bank could foreclose on you.

You could invest in art, antiques or jewelry, but try turning any of it into cash very fast unless it belonged to Jacqueline Kennedy or Princess Diana. And not only can art, antiques, and jewelry depreciate, they can be stolen, broken, burned or lost.

You can stash your money under your mattress, but it doesn't earn interest and inflation eats up its value. Or worse, a burglar finds it or the mattress catches on fire.

And the final slap in the face is that by the time you're old enough to collect social security, there might not be enough money left in the social security fund. So, forget thinking that you would be happy if you had just had financial security. There is no such thing.

But how and where do you draw the line between enjoying your life now and planning for you and your family's financial future? Let's say, for example, that you want to live in a comfortable home, drive a sports car, wear fashionable clothing, eat in trendy restaurants, travel and stay in nice hotels. This all takes lots of money. If you use all your money to enjoy your life now, what happens if there isn't anything left when you're too old to make a living? Not a pretty thought.

The answer is, do everything in *moderation*. Indulge now in those luxuries that will make your life richer. This includes purchasing beautiful objects that enrich and enhance your life as well as enjoying pleasurable experiences that make day-to-day living more exhilarating.

A silly reason to spend money is to impress other people, to control other people, or to try to make oneself happy because of some inner deep unhappiness that needs to be dealt with in some other way. Just as lives are not to waste, money is not to waste either. Use it wisely.

Always save and safely invest as much money as you can so that you don't have to worry about the future. Worrying about money is self-defeating because it saps you of the physical and emotional energy you need to *make* money. Work on feeling good about yourself and having control over your life. You will automatically feel confident about your ability to take care of yourself financially.

Accept That You Are Aging

There are some advantages to aging other than senior citizen's discounts. The biggest advantage is the peace of mind that comes from *accepting* that the world has always been and always will be full of problems; that you are only human and can only do the best that you can; that you may not possess great physical beauty, riches, nor a genius IQ; that you may not achieve the greatness you aspired to in your youth; that you are lovable only to those to whom you are special and that's okay; that nothing great is really expected of you; that the only expectations of you are the expectations that you create yourself; that you don't have to be something that you are not; and that you can finally get to relax and enjoy your life.

❧ *With acceptance comes love.* ❧

Chapter 11

Choose Not to Be a Victim

Take Control of Your Life

A few months ago my husband and I were walking down a street in Venice, California where a lot of transients hang out. One alcoholic said to us, "Can you spare a cigarette?"

Harvey answered, "I don't smoke."

The man said, "Well, how about some spare change?"

Harvey answered, "Why don't you get a job?"

The man replied, "I can't. My father beat me when I was growing up and that's why I'm all screwed up."

It seems like everyone likes to blame others for their own weaknesses and failures. Remember how the Menendez brothers became victims of their father's abuse when they tried to explain why they brutally murdered their parents? Remember how O. J. Simpson became a victim of Nicole when he said that it was Nicole who had abused him and a victim of the police when he accused the entire Los Angeles Police Department of framing him?

When the police interview criminals who have just committed a crime, it's common for the criminals to blame their accomplices for talking them into committing the crime. Even cold-blooded murderers think of themselves as victims of abusive parents or victims of society. It is this victimization mentality that usually justifies the horrendous crimes they commit.

If you *choose* to be happy, then you must *choose* to be in *control* of your life. You are the master of your own destiny. You must take full responsibility for each and every one of your actions and reactions. If you choose to continue being a victim of someone or some circumstance, you are sabotaging your own happiness.

Develop Resiliency

Steven Wolin, M.D. and Sybil Wolin, Ph.D., authors of *The Resilient Self: How Survivors of Troubled Families Rise above Adversity*, say everyone can develop the following resiliencies:

- "Insight. The mental habit of asking searching questions about you and those around you and giving honest answers. It begins in childhood with an intuition that family life is troubled, deepens into knowing the extent of those problems, and ripens into a mature understanding of oneself and others."

- "Independence. Getting emotional distance from the sources of our pain and mastering hurt feelings. Ultimately, separating oneself from the troubles in the family and in other close relationships."

- "Relationships. Actively searching for and cultivating alternative caring relationships. If one parent is abusive, for example, seek nurturing from the healthier parent—or from other family members, friends, a neighbor, teacher, scout troop or religious group."

- "Initiative. Carving out and mastering tasks not necessarily related to the sources of your problem, such as hobbies, skills and chores. Sometimes tackling the very responsibilities parents have failed to meet, such as caring for younger siblings, can provide a particularly empowering kind of strength."

- "Creativity. Transforming the ugliness in your life into beauty through, for example, art or athletics."

- "Humor. Seeing the comic in the tragic."

- "Morality. Engaging in activities of conscience—helping others in your family or community—which also makes you feel better about yourself."

Other researchers add that, in general, resilient people: accept the fact that life comes with hardship and pain; try to make an honest assessment of their problems rather than deny them; avoid wallowing in self-pity or a sense of victimization; see adversity as a challenge they can handle rather than an overwhelming threat; and deal constructively with their difficulties instead of sinking into pessimism and despair.

Use Your Victimization to Help Others

Certainly there are those in our society who *are* victimized by others. I can't deny that if you have been the victim of a crime, you *are* a victim. However, if you dwell on being a victim for the rest of your life and refuse to let go of what happened to you and move on with your life, you become a victim of not only the crime, but of your own thoughts.

The old saying that "Time heals all wounds" is true, but just because a wound heals doesn't mean it won't leave a scar. A scar is a constant reminder of what happened and what could happen again. If you *choose* to be happy, you will stop focusing on your scars and start thinking of ways that you can turn your negative experiences into positive ones. For example, John Walsh turned the abduction and murder of his son, Adam, into *America's Most Wanted*, a television show that is responsible for apprehending hundreds of wanted criminals.

Be Aware of Your Patterns

If the same thing keeps on happening to you over and over again, if you go from relationship to relationship, job to job, if you are always the victim and nothing ever works out—take a good look at yourself. It couldn't possibly be a coincidence that so many situations turn out the same.

Perhaps it's just your choices of people and jobs. Or maybe there is something in your personality that brings out the worst in other people. Maybe there are things about you that need changing. You can't *always* be a victim—maybe once in awhile—but not over and over again.

Listen to What Others Tell You

Sometimes people give you clues as to why other people are rejecting you or acting a certain way toward you. Don't get defensive. Realize that you are just human. Try to see how you affect other people. Aspire to be the best human you can, which involves self-examination and change.

I know people well into middle-age who still see themselves as victims of their own bad luck. Examine your own behavior to see what it is *you* are doing that causes this pattern of bad luck.

> ❧ *If you are not winning at the game of life,*
> *maybe you should reassess how you play the game.* ❧

Ask Yourself "What Am I Doing Wrong?"

Perceiving yourself as a victim is a poor excuse for not wanting to accept responsibility for your actions. No matter what has happened previously in your life, blaming someone else for your unhappiness or failure to achieve what you wanted to achieve will make you unhappy.

Diane used to be an upper middleclass housewife with a successful husband, a lovely home, two beautiful children, and lots of friends. After her divorce, she floated from relationship to relationship and from job to job. She seemed to purposely create arguments that alienated the only true friends she had left. It was always her ex-husband's fault, her fiancé's fault, her boss's fault, her coworker's fault, her children's fault or her friend's fault. Even her children didn't want to have anything to do with her anymore.

Diane saw herself as a victim. She never once asked herself or anyone, "What am I doing wrong?" She refused to accept that the cause of her problems was her own behavior.

The last time I ran into Diane she was carrying a duffel bag and wandering around a mall. I suspect she was homeless. Remember, what you think you are is usually what you become. Diane saw herself as a victim. It was a self-fulfilling prophecy. She became a victim.

It's Not Your Parents' Fault Anymore

Everyone comes from a dysfunctional family. It's just that some families are more dysfunctional than others. Your parents only taught their children what they had learned, just like you can only teach your children what you have learned. Unhappy people always remember the bad things that happened to them in their childhood but rarely remember the good things. Happy people forget the bad things and only remember the good things. To blame your parents for your unhappiness and lack of accomplishment is to see yourself as a victim.

Bad Memories Are Toxic

Of course, if you are really a victim of extreme physical, sexual and emotional abuse and are haunted by broken records and memories of past injustices that someone did or said to you, you need to get professional help.

Since the person who has hurt you probably doesn't care or is oblivious to the pain that he is still causing you, blaming and holding grudges doesn't hurt him, it hurts you. It is necessary for you to *accept and forgive* what has happened in the past and move forward.

    ❧ *If you* **choose** *to be happy,* **choose** *not to let any negative memories poison the quality of your life.* ❧

Refuse To Be an Enabler

Ask yourself if it is really the other person who is causing your unhappiness or if *you* are *causing your own* unhappiness.

Alan's wife, Fran, holds him hostage. She threatens to turn their five-year-old little girl against him and sue for custody if he leaves her. She refuses to work or do anything productive with her life and is always conveniently sick in bed.

He showers her with sympathy and has become Fran's *enabler*. Alan needs to deal with his own self-esteem issues and get the courage to leave Fran and fight for the right to be with his daughter.

If someone is making you into an *enabler*, it is because you fear losing him. You are actually afraid of him. How can you be happy when you are afraid of the very person you are supposed to share the rest of your life with?

Refuse To Be a Victim of an Abusive Relationship

No one should ever have to put up with emotional, verbal, physical or sexual abuse. First, get professional counseling to see if there is any possibility that you can change your partner's abusive behavior. If your partner won't or doesn't stop the abusive behavior after counseling, and if the relationship is causing you pain and anguish, it's time to end that relationship.

Realize that the abuser is sick. It is not your job to make a person like this well. The statistics have shown that abusers continue to abuse in relationship after relationship. Let go. It was a bad choice to be with this person. Forgive yourself. Don't keep on punishing yourself. Accept that you are a worthwhile person despite what this person has made you feel about yourself. You can make it on your own. Whether or not you ever find another relationship is irrelevant. Your self-esteem is the most important possession you have.

> ❧ *It is the ultimate rape of another person to take away his or her self-esteem.* ❧

What if you have children? Granted, children take divorce hard. However, growing up in a home where parents don't love each other anymore or parents hurt each other is even more damaging. Staying together for the sake of the children is just being a martyr.

Spousal and child abusers usually have a history of spousal and child abuse in their families. This behavior is a combination of genetics and early childhood learning. Abusers are genetically unhappy people with very low self-esteem. The worse they can make you feel about yourself, the better they can feel about themselves. If they are verbally, emotionally and/or physically abusive to you, they can destroy any self-esteem you might have. The goal of abusers is to make you feel so weak, so helpless and worthless that you will never leave them because you have no confidence in your ability to take care of yourself.

When Julie and her ex-husband went for marriage counseling before they separated, he used to say to her, "Prove you love me" over and over again. No matter what she told him and no matter what and how much she did for him, there seemed to be nothing she could do that could prove to him that she loved him. In his mind he didn't believe anyone could love him because he knew his innermost thoughts were unkind and unlovable. He thought that if he made enough money he would be able control people and then they would be *forced* to love him.

Abusers don't like to be rejected. When you are finally strong enough to leave an abuser this person will be furious with you and think of nothing else but punishing you for not loving him anymore. He will hate you for being the one person that he cannot control. He will seek the ultimate control in his revenge.

So, how do you get unstuck in an abusive relationship without ending up like Nicole Simpson? *Choose* to be happy. Refuse to be a victim. Once you refuse to let an abuser victimize you, he or she will scorn you, but eventually move on to find a new victim. It's easy for abusers to find new victims because abusers are usually very charismatic people. If they are wealthy, it is much easier for them because new victims love to be taken care of financially.

Okay, so you've got three kids, no money, and your husband is abusive. What are you supposed to do? First, *choose* not to be a victim. Next, *accept* that people rarely change their patterns. It has been proven that wife beaters are repeat offenders. First, they beg for forgiveness and then they promise never to abuse again. Once they have regained their partner's trust, they resume the same old abusive behavior. Just as it has been proven that most criminals, once let out of prison, become repeat offenders and end up back in prison again, most abusers continue to abuse. The longer you deny your situation the harder it becomes. And finally, *get help!* There are many agencies and services in your area that can help you get away from your abusive mate and get your life restarted.

Refuse To Be a Victim of Your Addictions

I believe that addictions are products of genetic unhappiness and/ or of an unhappy childhood. People who are genetically happy report having wonderful, happy childhoods and seem to have no addictions. People who come from unhappy families seem to have substance abuse problems and eating disorders.

People give in to their addictions because they want immediate gratification. They are unwilling to endure the discomfort of self-denial. They refuse to exert self-control. They refuse to take responsibility for their problems because it is easier to not have control over their lives. This is a symptom of low self-esteem and unhappiness.

In his book, *The Origin of Everyday Moods*, Robert Thayer, a psychologist at the California State University at Long Beach, claims that people use food to avert depression and to keep a good mood from slipping away. Participants in a weight loss program kept a diary of how they were feeling before and after they ate. When these people felt relaxed and happy in the company of family and friends, they reached for chocolate and other sweets even though they weren't hungry at all. "I strongly suspect that they began to indulge when they sensed a slight decrease in their happiness," says Thayer. "In such conditions, eating can be almost like a drug to perpetrate and enhance good feelings."

Yvette is addicted to sweets. She is extremely overweight and her cholesterol is over 300. She knows that she must stop eating so many sweets and exercise more if she doesn't want to have a stroke or heart attack, but she refuses to do anything about it. She is unwilling to deny herself immediate gratification.

I asked her "Why?"

She said, "I don't know."

Yvette is self-destructive because she is genetically unhappy and was raised in an unhappy family. Like most unhappy people, she perceives herself a victim of her parents. She will only overcome her addiction to sweets and lose weight when she *chooses* to be happy and stops blaming her parents. She needs to stop using her childhood as an excuse for her lack of willpower. She needs to let go of the past.

Tommy is 30 years old and has been in and out of drug rehab programs since he's been a teenager. He is adopted and I am sure that at least one of his biological parents is or was genetically unhappy and has or had similar addictions. His adoptive parents are a lovely couple that has ruined their lives trying to straighten Tommy out. Tommy will not be strong enough to be drug or alcohol free for any length of time until he *chooses* to overcome his genetic unhappiness. He sees himself as a victim of his biological parents because they abandoned him—and victims *never* get over their addictions.

Addictions don't necessarily have to be to substances. They can be to people. Elaine is addicted to relationships with unavailable men. For the past five years she has been in a relationship with an older married man who has made it clear to her that he will never leave his wife for her. He even encourages her to go out and date and find someone to marry. Elaine refuses. She is comfortable being second best. She is happy being unhappy. She is afraid to break up with this man because she is afraid no one else will love her. Elaine is addicted to this man's self-serving love. When I tell her that she is wasting the best years of her life, she says, "I know. The reason I'm so messed up is that my parents are so screwed up." Elaine perceives herself a victim of her parents.

You can even have an addiction to negative news and violence. In this instance, you see yourself a victim of a deteriorating society.

In order to break any addiction, you must finally decide that you want to be happy and that you *deserve* happiness. You must realize that the quality of your life is contingent on your good mental and physical health and that, in order to have good health, you must overcome your addictions. Most importantly, you must *choose* not to be a victim.

Addictions are an excuse for not wanting to grow up. People who refuse to do anything about their addictions are looking for an excuse not to be responsible.

🐚 *There are no addictions that are too strong to overcome; there are only people who are not strong enough to overcome them.* 🐚

Refuse To Be a Victim of Your Job

You have one life to live. How sad to find yourself at the end of your life only to realize that you have spent it doing something you hated doing. Don't wait that long. Do whatever it is you need to do so that you can wake up tomorrow morning looking forward to how you are going to spend your day.

Quit your job. Find another profession. Go back to school. There are many career counseling services that will help you find the career that is best suited for you. Trained counselors will guide you to take the right courses and help you find employment. If you need the money—most of us do—find a way to train for another job while you still keep the same job.

Once you take that first step, it's like a domino effect. Every action has a reaction. Before you know it, you'll be on the path to a new career. But, be realistic. If you weigh 300 pounds and can't keep time to music, don't aspire to be a ballet dancer.

Refuse To Be a Victim of Your Age

Every time you think that you're too old to change, remember that Grandma Moses started painting in her late seventies. Kiki is 52 years old and decided to go back to school a few years ago and become a lawyer. She is now working as a district attorney. Larry owned an executive search company and supported his wife and children for many years. He dreamed of becoming a teacher, so first his wife went back to school and got her law degree. Now she is supporting him while he goes to school to become a teacher so that he can fulfill his dreams.

If you think you are old, you are old. If you think you are young, you are young. Remember that each generation is at least 10 years younger physically and mentally than the generation before it.

Max is well over 65 years old and still works full time and plays tennis several nights a week. He has more mental and physical energy than most people in their twenties. The other day we were sitting in a restaurant and watched as this elderly couple found a table. They were both bent over with osteoporosis and obviously had never exercised.

Max said, "I wonder if people think that just because they get old that they're supposed to look and act old?"

I looked at him with his youthful clothes and spirit and was once again reminded that:

❧ *Age is not a number, it's an attitude.* ❧

Refuse To Grow Old

Most of us fear growing old. We fear being alone in old age. We fear not having enough money in our old age. We fear getting sick. We fear the pain of dying and the absence of life. We fear losing our youthful looks. We fear losing our minds. We fear losing our mates. If we are alone, we fear not finding a mate to spend our older years with. We fear we will not be able to take care of ourselves. We fear that our children will abandon us and not take care of us.

Conquering the fear of aging is like conquering any other fear. You fear the unknown. You fear what you have no control over. Thus, learn about aging. Know what the positives are. Know what the negatives are. Know how to plan your life so that you can live as comfortably and securely as possible in your later years.

In order not to fear growing old, you must begin taking control of your life now. One way to look forward to growing old is to make plans for how you want to spend your time after you retire. Just sitting around doing nothing but waiting to die is unacceptable. Plan to travel the places you have always wanted to go. Plan activities and hobbies you have always wanted to do. Move to a new place and meet new people. Keep your body as young as possible by practicing good preventative medicine. A part time business or part time job will help keep you mentally alert and physically active. Hopes and dreams should never end. Never stop learning. Exercise your mind and body. Stay involved in life and causes.

Focus on the good things about aging. Admittedly, these are few and far between but let's try to be positive:

- Senior citizens discounts

- Medicare

- No body odor

- You don't care whether someone likes you or not.

- You don't get embarrassed easily.

- You're not worried as much about your looks because you finally realize that nobody really cares anyway.

Overcome Your Physical Limitations

I was in the movie theatre a few weeks ago feeling sorry for myself because the herniated disc in my neck was really hurting me. I was sitting across the aisle from a woman in her early to mid-thirties who was talking to an elderly woman in front of her while waiting for the movie to start. The younger woman was alone and obviously had a nervous system disorder that caused her to shake and have involuntary movements. She was having difficulty holding a box of popcorn. She was telling the older woman that she had multiple sclerosis and that sometimes it was so painful that it was unbearable. Her insurance didn't cover the entire cost of the medication that she needed to relieve the pain so she had used up all of the credit on her credit cards to buy her prescription pain relievers. She operated a day care center and was smiling when she told the older woman how she was still able to hold and rock the babies. The moral of this story is that there is always something productive you can do with your life no matter what kind of condition you are in.

Stephen Hawking, a Professor of Mathematics at Cambridge University, has had a scientific career that has spanned over 40 years. His books and public appearances have made him an academic celebrity and a world-renowned theoretical physicist. Almost as soon as he arrived at Cambridge in 1962, he started developing symptoms of Lou Gehrig's disease, a type of motor neuron disease which caused him the loss of almost all of his neuromuscular control. Despite the fact that he has absolutely no physical abilities—he can't even speak—he has created brilliant works on theoretical cosmology and quantum gravity and has won many scientific medals and awards.

If you want to be happy and successful, you have to challenge both your mind and body. It's easy to make excuses why you can't do something. You are sick, you have a headache, a stomachache, a backache, or you are just plain too tired. And it's usually people who use these ailments who are always unhappy.

In order to be happy you must take control of your body. Don't let it control you. Don't be your own enabler. Don't make excuses and blame others for your own laziness or misbehavior.

Refuse To Be a Victim of Discrimination

Just as we have to let go and forgive our parents, so we have to let go and forgive society. Once upon a time blacks were slaves, Jews were put in concentration camps, and women didn't have the vote. But it's now the 21st century and most intelligent people judge other people not on the color of their skin, but on the content of their character.

There are plenty of African Americans, Jews, women, and other minorities who have proven that they can be successful. Blaming your lack of success on the fact that you are a minority is like blaming your lack of success on your parents.

Yes, there is such a thing as inequality. Yes, there is racism and bigotry. The Klu Klux Klan really does exist. But there are still plenty of opportunities out there for everyone. Stop making excuses and go find them.

Refuse To Be a Victim of Your Circumstances

"I'm physically sick, I'm mentally sick, I have bad luck, I was born into the wrong family, my parents screwed me up, and . . . " If you are always a victim, you are self-absorbed. You believe that everyone and everything in the Universe is out to victimize you. Do you really believe you are so important that everyone wants to spend his or her lives trying to screw you up? Rest assured, everyone is too busy worrying about his or herself to worry about you.

Take Responsibility for Your Own Life

Happy people have a sense of control over their lives. When you finally refuse to be a victim and take responsibility for your successes as well as your failures, you will be another step closer to finding happiness.

If you have a pattern of one relationship after another, one job after another, one apartment or house after another—stop blaming others. Instead, take a long, hard look and see what it is that you are doing that is causing this to happen.

Chapter 12

Don't Compare Your Life to Others

The Grass on the Other Side of the Fence Could Be Astroturf

Are you making yourself miserable by thinking that someone else is happier and more successful than you are? It's basic human nature to think that other people have more than you have and live a better life than you do. I used to compare myself to others, convincing myself that their lives were happier than my life. Perhaps that is and was true. But to judge your life by envying what other people have and focusing on what you don't have guarantees your unhappiness. If you *choose* to be happy you must focus on all the good things that you do have and acknowledge the negatives in your life *only* if you can change them.

We are constantly bombarded with commercials, television programs, magazine ads, billboards and movies in which the beauty and lifestyles of the rich and famous make us feel inadequate. The cosmetic companies claim that if we just rub on this new cream our wrinkles and our cellulite will disappear and our jowls will regain their elasticity and we will look like Cindy Crawford and live happily ever after. Men are told that if they take steroids, pump iron, and rinse their hair with For Men Only, they will look like Brad Pitt. We feel that we are not good enough if we don't measure up to these unrealistic images.

More men and women of all ages than ever before have eating disorders. Those who choose to believe they, too, can become perfect human specimens take life-threatening drugs and herbs, diet to excess, exercise to exhaustion, and undergo painful and expensive plastic surgery in order to look like the celebrity of the month. Those who can't or won't compete in the world of beauty resign themselves to a life of junk food and daytime talk shows until they grow so fat that they have to call the fire department to get them out through their own front door.

The media flaunts our lack of success in our faces, publishing the astronomical net worths of such super-achievers as Oprah Winfrey and Warren Buffett. Our expectations of our mates, our children, and ourselves become unrealistic. How can we feel good about our seemingly trite achievements when we are forced to compare ourselves to such successful people?

❧ Accept Your Own Limitations. ❧

The answer lies in your *acceptance* of your own limitations. First, accept credit for all the things you *can* do well. Next, acknowledge the things you *can't* do well. If you are to find happiness, you must make peace with who you are and what you are capable of doing. You might not be able to write like Tom Clancy, but you can do charity work and help people less fortunate than you. You might not be able to sing like Barbra Streisand but you are such a good salesperson that you are able to sell ice to an Eskimo.

The quest for youth, beauty, money, fame and power has blinded us from the true values of life. It is as if we think that the more of these qualities that we possess the happier we will be. *Wrong!* You go to a plastic surgeon and get rid of those outer symbols of unhappiness—the down-turned mouth, the sagging face, the bags, the scowl lines—but it will all be in vain if you don't give your inner thoughts a facelift too.

Like it or not, you are transparent. Your real self and inner thoughts show through your skin, eyes and body language.

❧ There is no hiding who and what you **really** are. ❧

Can Youth Bring Us Happiness?

In our society, youth is admired, middle-age is invisible, and old age is something we fear. Unfortunately, aging is a natural process of life and you are either going to get old or die young—take your pick. You can have your skin pulled, tucked and peeled. You can have your fat sucked out and your lips shot full of fat or collagen. You can have your hair dyed and plugs of hair transplanted into your scalp. But the bottom line is that we are all aging from the moment we are born until the moment we die. Never lose the child inside you. Find joy in simple pleasures.

❧ Youth will not bring happiness, but youthful thoughts will. ❧

In previous generations, the lifespan was shorter. Nature only intended our bodies to last long enough to reproduce offspring and raise them until they were self-sufficient and able to reproduce themselves. But mankind has outsmarted Mother Nature by increasing our lifespan with modern medicine. How we *choose* to spend these extra years of life and how we *choose* to view and accept the aging process is directly proportionate to our potential happiness.

Think back to when you were younger. Were you happier? My guess is probably not. When you were a child you couldn't wait to grow up so your parents couldn't tell you what to do anymore. You lived for your parents' approval. You feared disappointing your parents with a bad report card. You feared being punished for telling a little lie or sneaking a candy bar before dinner. You were forced to eat your veggies even though you hated them. Other kids teased you because you were too fat or too skinny or had buck-teeth or big ears. If only you were grown up you would be happy.

When you were a teenager you were plagued with acne, or your parents imposed a curfew on you, or you were "grounded" for talking back. Many of you fought with popularity issues and were extremely vulnerable to rejection from your peers. Everything embarrassed you. Your raging hormones played havoc with your emotions. If only you were grown up you would be happy.

When you were in your twenties you were too busy searching for an identity and making enough money to pay your own rent. If you got married in your twenties you were arguing over silly things with your mate. If you didn't get married, you were obsessed over finding a mate. If only you could find a mate—your soul mate—you would be happy.

In your thirties you are always busy trying to work and make ends meet. If you have children, you are always exhausted trying to be a good parent and make a living at the same time. If only you or your mate could get a job as a CEO of a company and make a six-figure salary you would be happy.

In your forties and fifties you are the "sandwich generation." You are busy trying to take care of yourself and your mate, not to mention your screwed up children and aging parents. To add to that, it has been increasingly difficult for you to make a living because the job market and the business climate have changed. You are always worried about money or your health or your children or your aging parents or losing your job or your business. If only you could win the lottery you would be happy.

In your sixties you are so busy trying to keep your body from falling apart and making enough money so you can retire that you don't have enough time to be happy. In some cases your children are older and they still can't take care of themselves and your parents are still alive and getting more helpless by the minute. You worry every day about who is going to take care of you when you get old. If only you could run away and find some utopian island where all you had to do was play golf you would be happy.

In your seventies and beyond, you are unhappy about your health, the things you wish you could have done "if only," your mate who died too young, and your adult children who forget to call you.

It is clear that youth alone cannot bring you happiness. Each stage of your life brings with it a new set of problems that must be overcome. It is impossible to overcome all of your problems because the act of living is the act of solving problems. If you think that solving all of your problems will bring you happiness, you are wrong.

❧ *Choose To Be Happy **in Spite of** Your Problems* ❧

Can Beauty Bring Happiness?

Society tells us that if we are beautiful females we will be happy. Prince Charming will come and buy us a Mercedes and a house in Malibu and we won't have to work anymore and all we have to do is go shopping at Neiman Marcus. If we are handsome males, some beautiful girls with very rich fathers will fall in love with us and their fathers will make us partners in their businesses and buy us Porsches.

Wrong! With beauty comes the pain of thinking that people only love you because you are pretty, that they don't even know or care about what's inside you. The aging beauty has not needed to learn other life skills and is often the unhappiest of all. No, beauty in itself cannot bring you happiness.

But in reverse, happiness can make you beautiful. Actress Drew Barrymore is recently quoted as saying, "I just think happiness is what makes you pretty. Period. Happy people are beautiful."

Can Money Bring Happiness?

Of course we all think money buys happiness, that we will be happy if only we can win the lottery. But as we found out earlier, studies of people who had won the lottery found that after one year they were no happier than they were before they won the lottery. In some cases, they were even less happy. Sure, money will buy us that new house or car or vacation or jewelry that we've dreamed about, but no amount of money will buy you that feeling of peace and happiness. Nope. It's not money either that brings happiness.

Can Fame Bring Happiness?

Probably not. Some of the least happy and loneliest people in the world are the most famous. I once had a blind date with a producer who was working on a film starring a famous actress. He told me that while they were on location the cast and crew would go out together in the evening and have dinner, but the star would sit in her room alone. One night he asked her to dinner. She accepted. At dinner she confided to him how lonely she was because the others had not invited her to go with them. Apparently they thought she was too famous to be one of them.

If fame brings happiness, then why are so many celebrities unhappy? Princess Diana was the perfect example. First there was the fairytale romance and wedding—the kind that millions of women fantasize about. Then there were the homes, the travel, and the beautiful clothes. Certainly Princess Diana led a blessed life. And yet, she was miserable. Her husband wasn't faithful, she had an eating disorder, and she couldn't even go to the gym without being harassed by the paparazzi. It is clear that fame doesn't necessarily bring happiness.

Can Power Bring Happiness?

Maybe it is power that brings happiness? Did Sadam Hussein look so happy? Did Hitler really look like he was having a ball?

Having power over people makes them resent you and they eventually begin to hate you. It is hard to be happy when you know everyone really despises you and that they just want to be around you for what you can do for them. No, power doesn't bring happiness.

What *Does* Bring Happiness?

The whole is only as good as the sum of its parts, so if youth, beauty, fame, money or power can't bring happiness, all of these ingredients together will not bring happiness. So, what does bring happiness? Finding pleasure and enjoyment in each moment, no matter how big or how small that pleasure.

Right now I am reminded of how much pleasure I am deriving from writing this book. I cannot explain this to someone who has never tried to be creative, someone who has never gotten lost in his or her own thoughts. It is what artists call the *flow* and athletes call the *zone*. I don't feel that I am missing something by being at home. I wouldn't rather be lunching with the ladies at Spago, skiing in Deer Valley or shopping in Paris. I'm perfectly content all by myself, wearing sweats, no makeup, and working at my computer.

❧ *Acts of love bring the ultimate pleasure.* ❧

Inner Beauty Brings Happiness

You must possess inner beauty in order to be happy. This means that your thoughts, feelings, words and actions are all loving. To be truly kind and caring is to be beautiful. Once you have erased all the mean thoughts from your mind and wish well to everyone, you will find your inner beauty.

❧ *Once you find your inner beauty, you will find your happiness.* ❧

Try to find good in everyone and everything. If you focus on what is good in your life, your life will be good.

Yes, there are people who live what appears to be glamorous lives—lives that we probably cannot and will not ever enjoy. We are jealous. We are envious. Have you ever noticed that when someone is successful there are always people who want to find something terrible about the person in order to bring him or her down? Proof of this lies in the huge circulation of the *National Enquirer* and the *Globe*.

Share Your Good Fortune

Luckily we are fortunate enough to live in a world in which there is enough abundance for us all. Did you ever notice that the people who are the most successful financially are those people who share their good fortune with others? They participate in mentor programs and give generously to charities. I doubt whether all financially successful people have been blessed with great financial success because of their kind and giving hearts. Rather, it is their kind and giving hearts that are a result of learning that money does not bring happiness unless you use it to bring comfort and happiness to others.

If you resent other people's success and beauty, then you do not believe in abundance. You probably do not believe that there is enough prosperity to go around so that everyone can experience it in some degree. If you think that only a chosen few have success and beauty and that if you aren't successful and/or beautiful, you can never be happy, then you will never be happy. If you derive pleasure from the misfortunes of others whom you perceive to have more than you, then you will probably experience your own misfortunes. Life is like a boomerang—you get back what you put out.

Of course, jealousy is a natural human emotion. Feeling sorry for yourself because someone possesses something that you don't have is perfectly normal. Don't berate yourself for feeling inadequate or jealous. Rather, try to focus on what things make you happy about your life and what you can do to change those things that are making you unhappy.

Recently I got an interesting lesson in life. I was feeling sorry for myself because I was focusing on what I *didn't* have in my life and ignoring what I *did* have in my life. We know a lot of people who *seem* to have it all—money, success, love, family, good looks and so on. However, in a period of two weeks I found out that one man we know, a doctor, was being sued by 37 patients for malpractice, had lost his medical license, and was being indicted by the federal government for fraudulent interstate advertising. I recently learned that his wife had left him and he had become an alcoholic.

Another couple I know who live in a five million dollar home and have three lovely children had just gone from having a business with 300 employees to closing the doors of their business because they couldn't meet their operating expenses.

Then I was jealous that a business associate of my husband's had sold his business for a huge sum of money to someone and was just working for him to keep busy. I was watching the news and found out that both of them had just been arrested for selling stolen auto parts.

What I learned from all this was that if people look like their lives are going too well, there is probably something about their lives you don't know. Just because they are rich, beautiful and possibly famous does not make them happy. Ask them, as I have, and they will tell you it is so.

Sometimes it helps to compare ourselves with people who have less than we do in order to feel better about our own lives. For instance, this morning I woke up feeling frustrated over our financial situation and lack of a close family. I started analyzing the people I knew and what their problems were. In each case, although they might have more money or closer families than we do, they each had their own problems. Then I turned on the news and saw people enduring horrendous tragedies in their lives. It wasn't long until I realized what a total jerk I was. It became crystal clear to me that no one has a perfect life. Everyone has problems. That by allowing thoughts of what I didn't have or what I haven't achieved poison my mind, I was actually keeping myself from getting those very things I wanted. Those toxic thoughts were ruining the quality of my life in the here and now.

*❧ If you **choose** to be happy, stop dwelling on what others have and what you don't have and focus on all the good things about your life. ❧*

When Good Things Happen to Everyone Else but You

We're supposed to feel happy when good things happen to other people— and sometimes we do. For instance, Julie, a lovely woman whom I met recently, has a wonderful spirit despite the fact that her life has been difficult. She has a grown mentally-retarded daughter and has recently gone through a divorce. She works very hard and the stress of it all has gotten to her physically. About three months ago she woke up one morning and there was a brown cloud over one eye. This could have been a symptom of about 12 different diseases. I just learned that the condition is finally clearing itself up without surgery and she will be fine. I am totally happy for her.

Now, if she had called and told me she had just won 40 million dollars in the state lottery I would be thrilled for her, too. The only difference is that my mind would start thinking, "Life isn't fair. How come nothing like that ever happens to me?" It is not that I wouldn't wish her the good fortune; it is just that I would like to have the same good fortune myself. This thought process is not really jealousy. It is merely wishing you could have the same good luck as someone else. This is not grounds for thinking that you are an evil person. Evil would be if you killed her, stole her lotto ticket, and collected the 40 million for yourself.

If we *choose* to be happy, we must break ourselves of the habit of being jealous. But when we are jealous, we must stop berating ourselves for feeling such a human emotion. If someone else has more than we have it does not mean that person is a happier person than we are. It just means that he or she has more than we do (as we perceive it.)

Lest you think I am more than human, let me confess that I have recently felt pangs of jealousy. We were at a dinner party and a woman rushed in and flashed a 10 carat diamond ring that her husband had just bought for her. (I, of course, was wearing a wedding ring recycled out of 30-year-old diamond chips and re-melted gold.) I learned that her husband is a very successful attorney, they have a huge, beautiful home in Beverly Hills, she spends her days shopping Rodeo Drive and they had just come back from a trip to Europe.

Later I learned that this woman's sister-in-law had recently gotten an eight carat diamond ring and this woman had cried and screamed to her husband until he agreed to let her trade in all of her other jewelry in order to get this 10 carat ring so she that could outdo her sister-in-law. I also learned that she was upset that her ex-husband and his new wife had just built a 20,000 square-foot house and that she was terribly jealous because she only had a 10,000 square-foot house.

I realized that this woman could not be happy if she had a 100 carat diamond ring and a 40,000 square-foot house. I possessed something that she could never possess—inner happiness.

Very recently, I heard that this woman had just found out that she had cancer and had to undergo surgery and radiation treatments. I also found out that her mother had died very young of the same type of cancer.

❧ Life has a way of teaching you what you need to learn. ❧

There will always be people richer than you, better-looking than you, healthier than you, smarter than you, more successful than you and more talented than you. That is just the way life is.

If you are unhappy because you don't have as much as someone else, then you are creating your own unhappiness. It is only human nature to always want more than you have. So, logically, if you are never satisfied with what you have, you will never be happy. Thus, you must learn to be happy with what you do have if you *choose* to be happy.

The problem here is that if you are completely happy with what you have, you won't have any motivation to achieve more. This is a paradox. What do you do? Learn to accept the negative things about your life you *cannot* change and do something about the negative things about your life you *can* change.

Purpose Brings Happiness

The purpose of life is to perpetuate itself—ideally, to create a better world for each new generation.

❧ Every moment of your life is a precious gift.
Accept it graciously. ❧

In order to be truly happy you must create a purpose to your life that will, in some small way, contribute to the common purpose of life. If your purpose creates a better life for each new generation in some small way, then you have been successful.

Rima's Theory of Relativity

Your problems are only as important or as terrible as you *perceive* them. Remember the old saying, "I was upset because I had no shoes until I saw a man who had no feet?" Well, maybe the man with no feet felt blessed because he saw a man with no feet and *no hands*. Perhaps the man with no feet and no hands also felt blessed because he saw a man who was *blind*.

There will always be people in the world who have more than you and there will always be people in the world who have less than you. Unless you are that one poor unfortunate person who literally has the worst life of anyone else in the whole entire world, you are not in a position to feel sorry for yourself.

I realize that no matter how bad others might have it, your problems and unhappiness will still make you feel bad. But your problems and unhappiness are only as bad as you *perceive* them.

Chapter 13

Choose Your People Well

Do you question people's motives when they are nice to you? Do you think everyone is out to get you? If something is missing, do you immediately accuse someone of stealing it instead of thinking that you have just misplaced it? Are you always disappointed in people? Do you often feel hurt because someone didn't live up to your expectations? Perhaps you are being unnecessarily paranoid and making yourself unhappy.

Happy people *choose* to believe that most people are honest. Happy, but smart, people believe that most people are honest, but accept that, unfortunately, some people are dishonest. They will probably lie to you and/or try to cheat you out of something. But why punish all the other perfectly sincere people you meet? Being distrustful will only make you unhappy. You are only punishing yourself by not trusting.

To trust someone and then to be betrayed by him or her is very painful. Unfortunately, manipulative people with selfish motives *do* exist. How do you recognize these wolves in sheep's clothing?

Dishonest People

- Give you more details and information than you need to know in order to convince you of something.

- Try hard to look you in your eyes when they speak because they are overcompensating for the fact that every book they've read says that when people lie they cannot look directly into your eyes.

- Have expressions on their face that don't match their words.

- Get defensive if you question what they are telling you.

- Try to manipulate you.

- Find someone else to lie to if they can't get away with lying to you.

- Promise you results that are too good to be true.

- Try to impress you with their possessions and accomplishments.

- Drop names of celebrities that they know.

- Do not live up to their words.

- Talk more than they listen.

- Prove to you over and over again that they cannot be trusted.

- Try to talk you into something you don't want to do or buy.

- Bond to you too quickly without letting your relationship develop naturally.

- Talk about other people to you. (Rest assured they would talk about *you* to other people.)

- Make a point of professing their great honesty and sincerity.

What do you do when you meet people who exhibit any of the above traits? If you *choose* to be happy, avoid them like a laxative on a camping trip.

People to Ban from Your Life

"Me-Me" People are so self-absorbed that they don't notice that there are events going on in the world that don't relate to them. You could be giving birth to triplets in front of them and they wouldn't notice. They love to hear themselves talk, but they never listen.

My ex-boyfriend just called and said jokingly, "Let's talk about you instead of me for a change. What do *you* think of *me*?" Understandably, he's my "ex" boyfriend. Of course, he said he was just kidding, but I know better. Every time he calls, before I can say a word, he gives me a long drawn out rundown of everything that is happening in his life—which isn't much—including a few dates and how much money he made that week. I could have died from old age before he asked how I was.

Finally, when he runs out of breath, he asks, "So, what's happening in your life?" When I start to tell him, he says, "Well, I don't want to take up that much of your time and I have to get going now."

Are people who live alone so self-absorbed because they live alone or do they live alone because they are so self-absorbed?

The Drama Queen/King is always in crisis. "I'm in love with a gay man." "I'm in love with a married man." "I'm bisexual." "I'm bulimic." "I'm anorexic." "I'm an alcoholic." "I'm a drug addict." "I'm a compulsive gambler." "I'm a cross-dresser." "I have obsessive-compulsive disorder." "I have attention deficit disorder." "I have a co-dependent personality." "I'm a prostitute." "I lost my job." "My car was repossessed." "My phone was pirated and I owe $2000 to the phone company." "I lost my health insurance." "The IRS garnished my wages." "I'm in jail."

These people get into one predicament after another in order to get attention. When things are going well, they will create another crisis to sabotage their success because a life flowing smoothly doesn't create the chaos they need in order to get them the attention they crave.

At first, these people are entertaining. Why pay to see a movie when a phone call from these people can entertain you for free? The only problem is that these people will not only eventually drain you financially and emotionally, they will suck you into their life dramas. In an all out effort to be a good friend you will find yourself being frisked at the local jail and losing your house to a bail bondsman.

The Goody-Goody Two Shoes spends her life trying to make everyone like her. She does everything right. She never says "No." A Goody-Goody Two Shoes never walks across the street if the red light is flashing or tears off the tag that says "Do Not Remove" from her mattress. She will stay up all night baking brownies for the church bake sale and all day making sandwiches to give out to the homeless in the park. And, of course, the Goody-Goody Two Shoes will make you feel inadequate and guilty for not being as wonderful as she.

The Cynic sees the world as an awful place. Everyone is out to get him. No one can be trusted. This is the person who tells you what is wrong with everyone and everything and always attracts negative karma.

The Cynic spews out generalizations like, "With my luck…," "All men are . . . ," "All women are . . . ," and "Well, what did you expect from them?"

The Cynic doesn't realize that you get back what you put out. This is the person who makes self-fulfilling prophecies come true. The world is a very bleak place for the Cynic. If you let him, he will make the world bleak for you, too.

The Martyr finds happiness in being unhappy. Martyrs enjoy suffering. Of course, they will always find a very subtle way to make you feel guilty for making them suffer.

The Knot is an uptight person who is like a suitcase full of plastic explosives. You never know when it's going to blow up. In every photograph, The Knot is on the sidelines looking like their mother just died.

This person just won't let go and have fun. They inadvertently inhibit your spontaneity and make you feel guilty for feeling happy and having a good time.

The Braggart thrives on making you feel inadequate. Everything he has is the best. Everything he does is the best. Every word out of his mouth is an effort to make you feel bad about yourself and your life. He does this because he feels inadequate. If he can make you feel inadequate, it makes *him* feel adequate, which he never really feels he is.

This toxic person does not have your best interests in mind. He feels in competition with you at all times. Understanding why this person acts this way and having compassion for this person's feelings of inadequacy does not make it feel any better when he tries to make you feel bad. If you *choose* to be happy, eliminate this person from your life.

The Phony has spent her childhood reading the tabloids and watching *Lifestyles of the Rich and Famous*. She has spent so much time wrapping her package that she forgot to put anything inside of it.

The Phony usually looks and dresses like she's worth a million dollars but usually can't even pay the minimum on her credit cards. She's always on the lookout for someone to get money from so she can keep up her facade. She will always choose going to a social function where she could conceivably meet a person who can enhance her social status over visiting you in the hospital. If you can't help her in some way or fill up some time in her useless life, she won't have any use for you. Always remember, underneath the posh exterior of The Phony lies a Phony.

The Big Mouth loves gossip. When there is no gossip, The Big Mouth creates it even if it isn't true. The Big Mouth has a boring life and needs to create drama. Sometimes the gossip is malicious because she is usually a very jealous person. This person loves to give backhanded compliments and play two friends against each other. You often hear her make comments like, "What a beautiful wedding. How much do you think it cost?" "Do you think the marriage will last?" "Do you think her breasts are real?" "Don't you think she wears too much makeup?" "I promised her I wouldn't tell anyone so promise me you won't tell her I told you."

The Gigolo is a wolf in sheep's clothing who leads you to believe that he is a wonderful, kind and caring person. He is very charismatic and knows how to make you feel attractive. Once he gains your trust and moves into your home, he will do things like try to get you to sign your inheritance over to him, "to avoid estate taxes," of course. You will find that the Mercedes he drives is registered to some other woman in some other city. Of course, you won't find this out until a police car stops you and hauls you both into jail. That's when you find out that the diamond engagement ring he gave you was "borrowed" from a jewelry store. When you finally extricate him from your home, you will notice many precious items missing. You will also receive many phone calls from his past and future "fiancées."

The Wolfette is a female wolf in designer clothes who leads you to believe that she is independent and just looking for a fulfilling relationship. The first clue that a woman is a Wolfette is that she makes reservations for you to take her to dinner at the most expensive, trendy restaurant in your city. The second clue that a woman is a Wolfette is that she orders extra food when you take her out to dinner—"to take home to her poor, sick roommate." This, of course, cuts down on her market bills at your expense. The third clue is when she tells you that she just lost her job and she doesn't have enough money to pay her rent.

The Giant Octopus enters your life like the opening ceremonies of the Olympics. Then, little by little, he takes over your life. First, he tries to change your eating habits. Then comes changing the way you dress. Next, he is rearranging your furniture and moving in his possessions. Next, he will try to turn you against your mother, your father, your best friend, all your other friends, your children, your boss, your business partner, your Rabbi, your Priest—even your favorite television show. The Giant Octopus wants to control you. If you resist, The Giant Octopus will get mad and begin planning his revenge.

The Whiner will always find something to complain about. "I'm dying from the heat." "I'm freezing to death." "The humidity is frizzing my hair." "It's so dry my hair won't take a curl." "There's no breeze." "It's too windy." "It's too spicy." "It's too bland."

The Sour Grape can't finish a sentence without telling you about the stock he got talked out of buying that doubled in two weeks. Or about the home in Sedona he could have bought before real estate there doubled. Or about the woman he could have had if he hadn't blown all his money in bad stocks and real estate deals.

The Bore will bore you with every detail of another friend's marriage, where her children went to school, how brilliant they are and how much each of them make. You will be listening to stories of her distant relatives and her children for hours on end. She can't be sidetracked. You can try to trick her into talking about something else, but she will always return to the original subject and force you to listen. The Bore will still be talking to you long after you have left the room and shut the door.

The Know-It-All knows everything. There is no opinion other than his own. He is always right. He refuses to accept advice. He always know best. He has a great need to always prove that he is right. The Know-It-All is always looking for a good challenge so that he can prove that he is smarter than you are. As a matter of fact, his main goal in life is to prove how smart he is and how stupid you are.

The Controller sees people as possessions. He believes that controlling you gives him power. The Controller will try to make you feel ugly and dumb and incompetent so you will not leave him. He will force you to say and do things that you do not want to do. He will convince you that he is right and that you and everyone else in your life are wrong. Power is to The Controller as heroine is to a drug addict. The only way to get rid of a Controller is to disentangle yourself from the relationship immediately.

The Perfectionist is usually suffering from a form of obsessive-compulsive disorder. Jody lines up her cans in the cupboard by measuring the labels with a ruler to make sure they are exactly equal distance apart. Her house is impeccable. Once I came over and took a peak in the refrigerator looking for something cold to drink. When she noticed the fingerprints on the chrome handle she went ballistic, screaming and yelling at me. The Perfectionist will drive you crazy trying to live up to her expectations—and, of course, you never will.

The People Pleaser needs constant approval because she feels insecure. She needs others to tell her that she is attractive, sexy, bright, talented, good and moral. A People Pleaser likes to make lots of friends who are always complimenting her and making her feel good about herself. A People Pleaser does not feel good about herself unless other people are telling her how wonderful she is. She usually spends so much time pleasing other people that she has no time left over to develop other interests. The People Pleaser makes a good friend. The problem is that, in some cases, she is being a good friend to you only because she wants you to think that she is wonderful.

The Flake loves chaos and drama so she makes sure her life is filled with it. It makes her feel important and gives her an excuse for non-performance. The Flake is always late—if she does show up at all—and has no respect for your time. She never follows through. You can place a bet on the fact that if she says she is going to do something, she won't do it. A Flake likes being a Flake. If she didn't, she would do something about it. Being a Flake gives her an excuse for being a failure, which she always is; being a Flake gives her an excuse for being alone, which she always is; and a reason for being unhappy, which she always is. Always count on The Flake to expect you to be there for her when she needs you. Don't ever count on The Flake to be there for you.

The Sad Sack calls all the time to tell you how depressed he is. His life is miserable, but he seems to have the ability to pick himself up, dust himself off, and try again and again. However, being depressed is a way of life for him. He likes to hide his depression by being unbelievably happy when he knows that you know that underneath he is really depressed. This makes him think that people will think that he is wonderful for being able to act so "up" when he is so "down." Being unhappy seems to make him happy.

The Hippie uses his spirituality as an excuse to freeload. Hippies are often artists, writers or sculptors, however one rarely, if ever, sees any of his work. He is usually extremely charismatic and has a well developed ability to charm the opposite sex. The Hippie uses his free spirit as an excuse not to work. He doesn't seem to need a lot of money because he is very good at living off of other people. This is the house-guest from hell.

The Victim is always in some life crisis. She is broke, her boy-friend is abusing her, her car was stolen or repossessed, or she lost their job. It is *never* her fault. It is always the fault of society, the govern-ment, her boss, her boyfriend, her husband, her mother, her father, her third cousin twice removed. She blames her "bad luck" on whoever is convenient, never stopping to think that poor life choices are creating her bad luck. The Victim feels undermined and overwhelmed most of the time, which leaves her powerless and immobilized. If you allow The Victim into your life, you become a victim of The Victim.

The Sex Addict loves the immediate gratification that sex pro-vides. He usually can feel no love or compassion for another human being because he doesn't love himself. In some cases, he is constantly seeking out others' expressions of love because he feels so unlovable. In other cases, life is so meaningless for him and he is so shallow, that just feeling good sexually is enough to make him feel okay about him-self for that moment. If the Sex Addict is a male, he has learned to say anything in order to con a woman into having sex with him. If The Sex Addict is a woman, she has learned to be stoned in order not to take responsibility for her promiscuity. Unfortunately, with sexually trans-mitted diseases, this is a game of Russian roulette.

The Whore believes that her body is an object with which to barter for material possessions. She does not see another human being as hav-ing feelings, but as someone to take care of her needs. The Whore has no respect for her body. It belongs to whoever can pay for it. The Whore will tell you that she wants a normal life, a normal job and a normal mate. But people who have no respect for themselves have no respect for anyone else. The Whore will take all she can get from you and leave you either when you have no more left to give or someone else comes along who can give her more.

The Doormat is hard not to step on because he always seems to put himself right where he is sure to be stepped on. A Doormat feels comfortable being stepped on. He is never assertive. He will do anything you want him to do. He really doesn't have a mind of his own. Doormats are about as enjoyable to be with as their woven hemp counterparts.

The Addict drinks or takes drugs because being an Addict gives him an excuse for not taking responsibility for his life. The Addict does not want to be an adult. He always finds an enabler who believes she can save him. The only way The Addict is going to change is if he decides not to use drugs or alcohol as an excuse for not being responsible.

The User is the real estate agent that wants to be your friend because maybe you or someone you know might give her a listing. The screenwriter who thinks you might have a connection in "The Biz." The social climber that thinks you'll introduce her to the right people. The stockbroker who knows you have some wealthy friends.

The Attorney always knows more than you do. He always has a higher I.Q. than you do. He knows how to argue better than you do. The Attorney talks in words and terms you could never understand. The Attorney talks at you so fast you won't know what hit you (until you get the bill.)

The Intellect has an advanced degree and a stable of "published" friends. This person loves to go to the opera and the ballet and foreign movies—even if she is secretly bored to tears. The Intellect is clearly much brighter than you are, and thus, clearly much better than you. The Intellect is truly obnoxious.

The Wading Pool is so shallow that she can spend endless hours boring you with the smallest, most trivial details, like the party favors for a bridal shower. We assure ourselves that nobody could be that shallow. Then we listen to The Wading Pool discuss at length which belt to wear with which outfit and we realize that, yes, The Wading Pool is *that* shallow.

The Bully has learned that he can get anything he wants from people by intimidation. He will hit, shout, manipulate, trick or beat you into doing whatever he wants you to do. You know you have been bullied when you agree to do anything that goes against your better judgment.

The Prophet of Gloom is like Chicken Little running around screaming that the sky is going to fall. This person believes that there is no hope for mankind; that the stock market is going to crash; the real estate market is going to crash; that we are all going to die from some virus put into our water supply by some terrorist. The Prophet of Gloom believes that there is no hope for the youth of this country, that foreigners are ruining our country, and that our environment is completely polluted. He or she is afraid that a giant earthquake is going to destroy the earth or that a huge asteroid is going to fall to earth and blow our planet apart. The Prophet of Gloom believes in Armageddon.

The Fair-Weather Friend loves to call and use your time and ear to listen to her problems. However, if you have a problem, The Fair-Weather Friend is nowhere to be found.

The Lost Soul wanders around looking lost, searching for someone or something to make him happy. It rarely occurs to The Lost Soul that it would be nice if he tried to make someone else happy.

The Plastic Surgery Junkie can't stand the thought of looking less-than-perfect, much less enduring the curse of looking old. She runs from plastic surgeon to plastic surgeon having her face pulled, her nose bobbed, her breasts pumped up, her derriere lifted, her fat sucked out. Her lips have been injected with so much collagen that she can't even suck from a straw. The Plastic Surgery Junkie clearly has more self-esteem issues than you have time to listen to if you want to be productive and happy.

The Job Hopper is fired from job after job, but it is never his fault. It is always, "The boss had severe emotional problems" or "The people I worked with were jealous of me." You will get a stiff neck and a headache sitting on the phone for hours listening to the woes and complaints of The Job Hopper.

The Space Cadet walks around with a blank expression on her face, oblivious to the world. She could have been introduced to you umpteen times, but she never notices that you are alive. The Space Cadet is either very high on drugs or has had a lobotomy. This you don't need.

The Liar doesn't really believe that he is very interesting so he makes up stories to make his life sound more exciting. The Liar will entertain you with stories about all the times he went skydiving or the time he skied from the top of the Cornice to the base of the mountain without a ski lesson and without falling. Want to have some fun? Call a Liar's bluff. Take him to the top of the mountain and give him a "little push."

The Nervous Wreck creates her own stress. Everything is all too much for her. She loses everything and purposely leaves everything to the last minute. She usually talks fast and incessantly and has a tendency to make you even more nervous than she is. It doesn't matter whether she is high on caffeine, cocaine or naturally on fast forward, an hour with The Nervous Wreck will make you want to take a Valium.

The Cheater gets a thrill out of getting away with something he is not supposed to do. This makes him feel like he's put one over on you.

The Criminal feels that he is *entitled* to whatever he took, even if it is from his best friend or a relative. He feels power over his victims. If you hang around a Criminal you will either become a Criminal or a Victim. Neither one is a viable option for someone like you who *chooses* to be happy.

The Slob has a messy house, messy hair, messy clothes, a messy purse, and a messy car. If she keeps herself and her belongings a mess, rest assured the inside of her head is a mess too.

The Sadist is just plain mean. Underneath he feels inadequate and so everyone is a threat to him. The Sadist gets great pleasure from hurting other people. This does not exclude friends and relatives. If you are being hurt by a Sadist—run!

The Critic can find something wrong with everyone and everything no matter how perfect. The pasta is too bland, too spicy, too overcooked, or too raw. A girlfriend is too fat, too short, has a big rear-end, bow legs, spider veins, yadda yadda. When The Critic tries hard not to be critical about someone or something, there is this disingenuous look on her face and insincerity in her voice that says, "I'm dying to say something bad."

It is usually the person that finds the most flaws in others who *has* the most flaws. The Critic actually feels bad about her own flaws and tries to make herself feel better by criticizing others. She usually asks a few key questions like "Are you wearing that outfit on purpose?" or "What is that red, pus-filled thing on the tip of your nose?" The best way to handle a comment like this is to say, "Wouldn't you look better out there?" as you gently shove The Critic out your front door and close it firmly.

The Baby is the adult-child who still blames everything bad that happens in her life on her parents. She loves to talk like a baby. She chooses enabling mates and friends who treat her like a helpless baby. She likes to play sick for the same reasons that you pretended you were sick so that your mother wouldn't make you go to school and take that test you dreaded.

The Other Woman/The Other Man is the victim who settles for being second best. He or she seems to get a sick pleasure out of always being obsessed with an unavailable mate and seems to get an adrenaline high from the love triangle he or she has created. Deep in their hearts, they know they are going to get hurt in the end. They want to hurt themselves so they can say, "See, I always get hurt." It is a lack of respect for oneself. It is a way of sabotaging one's happiness.

So who's left? Granted, the pickings are slim. Most of us have elements of one or more of the above characteristics in our personalities. But, if we *choose* to be happy, we should choose joyful, successful, enthusiastic, honest, sincere friends who have the fewest of the above qualities and who make us feel good about ourselves.

A Sincere Person will:

- Not try to convince you of anything.
- Not tell you anything to impress you. This person's actions speak for them.
- Never let you down.
- Be modest about his or her accomplishments.
- Listen more than he or she talks.
- Prove to you over and over again he or she can be trusted.

Happiness and Unhappiness Are Contagious

Unhappiness is like a bad flu. If you intermingle with unhappy people, you will catch their unhappiness. Happiness is like a lucky charm. If you socialize with happy people, you will catch their happiness and good luck. Rich people have rich friends. Enthusiastic people have enthusiastic friends. Happy people have happy friends. It's that simple. If you want to be happy, *choose* happy friends!

Toxic People Keep You from Feeling Happy

If you *choose* to be happy, don't let anyone drag you into his or her misery. If someone tries to undermine your happiness you can rest assured that he or she is toxic. Toxic people pretend that they have your best interests in mind, but beneath their warm smiles and flowery words they wish you bad. Misery loves company. If they can make you feel unhappy, it makes them feel better about their own unhappiness.

Be a quick toxic-person detector. Whenever you meet new people, give them this Toxic Person Test before you let them enter your life. Be on alert for the following early warning signs:

- Nervous tics and mannerisms
- Incessant rambling that doesn't always make sense
- Complaining
- Uptight, guarded body language
- Not giving you your space
- Touching you inappropriately
- Facial expressions that don't match their words

Is a toxic person already poisoning your life? Toxic people:

- Give backhanded compliments. They tell you to your face how happy they are because you just met "Mr. or Mrs. Right." As soon as you leave, they call a mutual friend and express their concern. They are worried about you because they are afraid that Mr. or Mrs. Right is going to realize what a neurotic you are and dump you.
- Try to make you feel guilty about everything you do and say.
- Find fault with everything you do and say.
- Act too sweet. They tell you how much they care about you and

how much they want you to do well, but beneath their flowery words they want you to fall on your face because it makes them feel better about their own failures.

- Are always late. This is their way of letting you know that they think that their time is more important than your time.

- Always apologize for their bad behavior—then do the same thing to you over and over again.

- Are always victims. They are always angry or depressed about something or someone. Somebody is always out to do them wrong.

- Bend your ears with stories and details you couldn't possibly be interested in. They are unaware that you are totally uninterested because they don't care if you are bored to tears.

- Try to undermine your self-esteem by making you feel inadequate or incompetent.

- Try to make you feel wrong or stupid—or whatever it is they can make you feel—that makes them feel better about themselves.

- Pass judgment on you. They are usually the very same people who have committed acts that you should have passed judgment on (but didn't.) No one has a right to pass judgment on you.

- Complain constantly. They complain about the weather. They grouch about their work. They grumble about their mates. They fret about their children. They whine about their health. They find fault with their friends. If business is bad, they gripe about having no money. If business is good, they grumble about being too busy. If there is nothing to complain about, they complain about having nothing to complain about.

- Are negative. They will always find the worst in everyone and everything.

- Live from one soap box drama to the next. It's not just coincidence that they seem to attract one tragedy after another.

- Have not let go of their past. It is their mother's, father's, brother's, sister's, aunt's, uncle's, grandmother's, grand-father's, great grandmother's, great grandfather's, friend's, children's, babysitter's, neighbor's fault that they are so screwed up.

- Anorexic, bulimic, over-eaters, yo-yo dieters, prescription pill junkies, drug addicts or alcoholics. They can find things to be addicted to that aren't even physically addictive— exercise, sitcoms, married men, shopping.

- Profess their great love for you and then are too busy with some problem of their own to visit you when you are in the hospital.

- Go from one relationship to another. It is always the other person's fault.

- Go from one job to another. It is always the boss's fault.

- Move from one place to another. It is always the landlord's fault.

- Never remember your birthday.

- Have no idea they are toxic and don't care, either.

What if you just realized that *you* are a toxic person? Change! You can't be happy and be a toxic person at the same time.

Make an Asset and Liability List

Take an inventory of all the people you know, including your mate, family, friends, coworkers, casual acquaintances, people at your church or synagogue, people you work with in organizations, neighbors—anyone who affects your life.

Next, think about each person and decide what he or she adds to the quality of your life. For instance, Elizabeth makes me laugh and listens when I tell her if there is something really bothering me. Lynette snips at me and tries to make me feel stupid and really doesn't seem to have any interest in what is going on in my life. Obviously, Elizabeth is an asset to my life and Lynette is a liability.

Once you have divided everyone into an asset or a liability, set a goal to add more relationships that are assets to your life and decrease the number of people in your life that are liabilities. You will find that once you let go of the people who are toxic, people who are assets will automatically be drawn to you.

Limit Your Exposure to Toxic People

Having too many toxic people in your life is like inhaling too much secondhand smoke. So, what do you do when you realize that an old friend is toxic? Do you give up on her as a friend? Do you confront her and try to help her? Most of us have those "old friends" in our lives that we've outgrown. We keep them in our lives because we don't want to give up our ties to the past. But remember, if you *choose* to be happy, you can't live in the past.

I had a friend who I had been friends with for 30 years. Let's call her Michelle. She was a drama queen whose life was filled with catastrophes. I think the part of me that wanted to be unhappy was entertained by her calamities. She had so many traumatic events happen in her life that I was beginning to believe that she actually willed them to happen. She seemed to thrive on chaos and drama.

I was the stable one, always available for her; always willing to listen to her problems, come to her rescue, do her a favor, and pay for her when she conveniently forgot her wallet. I was there with her at the hospital for days on end when her older son was treated for lymphoma. I was there for her when her younger son was shot and killed by another teenager at a teenage disco. I even took her to the morgue to identify the body. I was there for her when she got fungus of the lung after the 1994 Northridge earthquake. I was the one who stayed up all night trying to stop the doctors from removing yet another lobe of her lung. I never got as much as a "thank you."

And then I was in the hospital with spinal meningitis and I needed Michelle. She wasn't there for me. She had every excuse in the book, but the bottom line is that she wasn't there for me. Not only did she never come to see me, she *never* even called to see how I was doing. It practically took being hit on the head with a sledgehammer to finally realize that she had *never* been there for me and *would never* be there. She was not on my team. She was using me. It finally sunk in that she was a profound negative influence in my life. I realized that she never made me feel good about myself. She only made me feel bad. It finally occurred to me that underneath her loving words she actually *enjoyed* making me feel bad.

It was my birthday—a big one. Having been admonished by me previously for not remembering my birthdays, Michelle sent a card that read as if it was from stranger I had just met. She did call to wish me a happy birthday in the morning. No birthday lunch, as I had done for her almost every year. I thanked her and made the mistake of asking, "What's going on with you?"

My birthday morning became a dissertation of how she was a victim (once again). At that moment, I realized that this woman cared about no one else but herself. She always said goodbye to me with a big hug and the words "I love you," but her actions did not match her words. I decided she was toxic and that I had to extricate her from my life.

She called several times after, but I wouldn't return her calls. She never tried calling or writing to find out why I was rejecting her friendship after 30 years. Perhaps she already knew. Perhaps she didn't care. Perhaps I was no longer useful to her. It is now clear that if she was willing to let a 30 year friendship go that easily, I really didn't mean much to her. I miss her in the same way a child misses a parent who abused him or her. But I *choose* to be happy and she was toxic to my life.

Several months later I ran into Michelle's other best friend. She told me that she had stopped being friends with Michelle because every time she saw or talked to her she left feeling bad. I was finally convinced that Michelle was toxic and stopped feeling guilty about never returning her phone calls.

Just recently I ran into a man who knew her socially and had some business dealings with her as well. He had stronger words for Michelle, like "She's the most evil person I have ever met."

It only took me 30 years to realize just how much this toxic relationship was poisoning my life. But the moment I *chose* to be happy and to end this relationship, my life opened up with fabulous new opportunities and new wonderful, loving, non-toxic friends.

Leading a mentally healthy life after you have been leading a mentally unhealthy life is uncomfortable at first. You are probably used to the excitement of the drama and the misery. It's kind of like the feeling you get when you stop smoking and start eating healthy and exercising. You miss those big greasy donuts and thick gravies that have been clogging your arteries and making you fat. But then you finally learn to really like the plain, fresh fruit and vegetables and grilled fish with no sauce. One day you are served something covered with cream sauce and you cringe with disgust. How could you have ever put something so unhealthy into your body? The same is true with friends. You will be totally amazed how you could have once have allowed someone so obviously toxic to poison your life.

Once you *choose* to be happy and get rid of all the toxic people in your life, your world will refill itself with new, healthier friends.

Choose Your Mate Well

I heard on the news recently that a couple was celebrating their 80th anniversary. They were both in their late nineties. The interviewer asked the wife, "What is the secret of the success of such a long marriage?"

She replied, "Pick a man with an even disposition."

This is such a simple, but true, statement. So many of us settle for mates that have personalities that we know are difficult to live with before we even say "I do." Perhaps we think they will change once we are married. Wrong! Most difficult people are difficult forever.

❧ *A leopard never changes its spots.* ❧

Ana goes from one miserable relationship to the next. She is living with a man who had just been released from a six-year sentence in a federal penitentiary for drug dealing and tax evasion when she met him. He is still on probation. Almost three years into this rocky relationship Ana admitted to me that this man is abusive. She wants to get away from him, but she's frightened that he will hurt her and he has her convinced that she cannot survive without him. Ana knowingly got involved with a man who was going to make her life miserable. Why?

Ana clearly has very low self-esteem and does not believe that she is worthy of anyone better. She has convinced herself that there is nobody any better out there anyway. She has not learned how to fend in the world financially for herself and has become dependent on this man. She is naive and believed him when he told her that he was just a victim of our corrupt government. She believed in the financial fairy-tales that this man told her.

Now she is stuck. She has no money of her own, no work experience and no place to live. She let him use her car and now it doesn't work. She seems to do this to herself over and over again.

If you *choose* to be happy, surround yourself with quality people who provide you with the loving kindness, nurturing and respect that you deserve.

Chapter 14

Refuse to Worry

Worry is a gnawing feeling inside of us that sabotages any possible enjoyment of life that we might have. It never leaves us. It taints our lives. We cannot worry and be happy at the same time. It is like eating sweet and crispy Frosted Flakes with sour milk.

Worry Can Be Genetic

A tendency toward nervousness or depression is at least partly inherited according to psychiatrist Klaus-Peter Lesch of the University of Wurzburg and his colleagues from the U.S. National Institutes of Health. The researches ran 505 men and women through standard personality tests in which they rated their agreement with statements such as, "I am often nervous and apprehensive" and "I feel a little anxious around wild animals even when they are locked up in strong cages." The scientists then took blood samples for genetic analysis.

Participants who scored higher on anxiety-related questions tended to have a shorter version of the gene that regulates serotonin, a brain messenger known to be crucial to a wide variety of behaviors, including eating and sleeping as well as mood.

This study is the first to uncover a small but significant link between pessimistic behavior, the tendency to be anxious, hostile, depressed and impulsive, and a gene that helps control how serotonin is used in the brain. Benjamin Greenberg, a psychiatrist with the National Institutes of Mental Health, was one of the study's U.S. researchers. He states that two-thirds of the volunteers had the short version of the gene, which predisposes these neurotic traits. He estimates that there are 15 still-unidentified genes that may play a role in making one person happy and another person sad in combination with environmental factors.

Worrying Will Make You Sick

There is much truth in the words of advice "You're going to worry yourself sick!" Peter, from whom my husband bought his business, was always worrying about money from the minute he woke up to the minute he went to sleep. He always denied himself life's pleasures in order to save money and increase his already very large bank account. Unfortunately, Peter got throat cancer. He eventually died, but even when he could barely speak and was in excruciating pain, he would call us if our payment to him was detained in the mail by one day. I believe Peter's obsessive worry over money caused a breakdown in his immune system, which allowed the cancer cells to invade his body.

Sybil also obsesses about the lack of money with which to retire. She worries constantly that she will not have enough money in the bank. She worries about whether she will be well enough to support herself when she is older. She's only 52 years old, but she now has angina and colitis. Her worrying probably caused or at least exasperated both of these conditions.

If you are a genetically unhappy person, the odds are that you spend a lot of time worrying. If there is something to worry about, you worry about it. You worry about not having children. You worry about your children when you do have them. How are you going to pay for their education? How can you keep them from being abducted by some child molester? Are they normal? Are they taking drugs?

You worry about pleasing your mate. You worry about your mate's health. You worry if your mate comes home a little late that he or she has been in a car accident. You worry if your mate is cheating on you. You worry about losing your job or your business. You worry whether you forgot to turn off the coffee maker before you left on your trip. You worry that your house is going to catch on fire. You worry that you are going to be carjacked.

And you defend your worrying by saying that if you don't worry about your old age and make a savings plan that you won't be able to enjoy a retirement. If you don't worry about your health, you won't exercise, eat right, and get a check up. If you don't worry about feeding your family, you won't get a job or go to your business every day.

But you cannot be happy and worried at the same time and so you must …

Take Control of Your Life

The more you are in control of your life the less you will worry. Always ask yourself "What if?" Imagine the worst possible scenario that could happen to you. Then, instead of worrying about it, take action. Make whatever plans you need to make in order to ensure that the worst case scenario you are imagining will never happen. Accept that worry accomplishes nothing. Do what needs to be done and then let it go.

Worrying is just fear of the future. You can't worry about the present because you are already experiencing it right now. You can't worry about the past because you already know what happened and you survived it (no matter how difficult it was) because you are still here. Because of this, you must realize that if you were strong enough to make it through all the years of crises you have gone through, you certainly must be strong enough to make it through all the years of crises still ahead. This, of course, is very simple in theory but very difficult to put into practice. Let's go through some of the common things you probably worry about and I'll show you why you should not worry about them.

Stop Worrying About Money

If you are constantly worrying about not having enough money, you are robbing yourself of the pleasure of enjoying your life in the here and now.

The older we get the more we have a natural tendency to worry about what will happen when we get really old. The dilemma is how to enjoy your life in the present without sacrificing the security of your future. Should you deny yourself the goodies of life that you would like to enjoy now so that you will have money in the future? Or, should you "live for today" and spend everything you have and enjoy it because who knows if you will be alive tomorrow? It's a Catch-22.

If you deny yourself the pleasures of life you desire now, you will resent your life and feel deprived and unhappy. If you indulge your desires and enjoy your life now, you must endure the worry of the future, which will make you unhappy. What's a person to do?

Make a list of expenses that are necessary. A list of purchases you *have to* make; purchases you'd *like to* make; and purchases that are *not necessary* to make. Before you spend on anything, ask yourself:

- Is this item, trip or luxury going to enhance my basic happiness or is it just going to be one more item stuck up on a closet shelf unused?

- Am I going to be upset on my deathbed and really feel I missed out on one of life's experiences because I denied myself this experience?

- What are the real reasons why I want to have this item or experience?

Decide to spend your money wisely on those things that give you the most pure and lasting pleasure in the present. Control your urges to purchase those luxuries that will only bring you fleeting pleasure and that will not truly enhance the quality of your life. Since financial security will bring some sense of inner peace to your life, it should be a part of your master plan for the future. If you *choose* to be happy, save what you can, stop worrying about the future, and enjoy your life. As in everything in life, practice moderation.

This, of course, is hypocritical to my advice, "Live each day as if it is your last." So, I would like to add a tag line:

*❧ Live each day as if it is your last,
but save some money in case it isn't. ❧*

No matter how much money you have, if you are a worrier, you are going to worry about not having enough money. The only difference between a poor person who worries about money and a rich person who worries about money is the actual dollar amount. Wealthy people worry about money as much as you. They just worry about bigger amounts of money.

❧ *It's not the lack of money that usually causes you to be unhappy, but rather the worry of the lack of money.* ❧

Life has a way of providing you with what you need. If you live right, think right, do all the right things to the best of your ability, opportunities will present themselves to you.

❧ *Worrying about what is going to happen to you tomorrow only ruins your enjoyment of today.* ❧

Make a Financial Plan

What are your goals for one year? Five years? Ten years? Twenty years? Thirty years? Retirement? If you worry about financial security and yet don't have a financial plan, it's like building a house without a blueprint.

- Create a realistic savings plan and stick to it. Every week or every month add money to your savings, no matter what. Make safe, prudent investments in stocks, bonds and mutual funds. Find a reputable broker and/or financial advisor who will help you set up your portfolio.

- "Just say no" to instant gratification. Sure, it's fun to buy pretty things, but most of the time we spend money on items that look great in the store display and we get home and they become just more "stuff" sitting on a shelf collecting dust. You will never reach your financial goals unless you save some money. And if you worry about financial security and yet throw away money on frivolous whims, then you are sabotaging your own happiness by causing yourself to worry.

- Create a spending plan according to priorities. The first priorities are essential living expenses, which include food, shelter, clothing, transportation, medical expenses, telephone bills, education, your savings plan, and so forth. The second priority is spending money on making more money—continuing education, advertising your new business, or upgrading your business computer system. The third priority is buying things that you need for your home that will make it into a better environment so that you may be more productive. Or, perhaps it is buying new clothes that will make you look and feel better. The fourth priority should be the goodies—a new car, fine artwork, exotic vacations, or expensive restaurants—but only if you can really afford them.

- Don't panic. If you have a setback and lose your job or business or have a financial emergency, don't revert into your old worry mode. Use your physical and emotional energy to think of new ways to create income. Do everything you can to make money—legal of course.

Stop Worrying About Your Health

If you are constantly worrying about your health you are actually going to "worry yourself sick." We are all born with a certain genetic predisposition to particular diseases and conditions. We are all vulnerable to accidents. The best you can do is:

- Take control of your health. Do everything possible to be as healthy as you can. In order to overcome your genetic tendencies, take care of your body—it's the only one you'll ever have. Exercise, eat right, don't take recreational drugs, don't drink too much alcohol, get plenty of rest, and try to alleviate as much stress as possible. Get regular medical checkups. Heart attacks, strokes and cancer can often be avoided by a healthy lifestyle.

- Educate yourself. If you worry that every little gas pain is a heart attack and every little mole on your skin is a melanoma you *are* worrying yourself sick and even qualify for hypochondriac status. On the other hand, if you ignore that little gas pain and it is a heart attack or you ignore that little spot on your back and it *is* a melanoma, you can be in big trouble.

The more you know about particular conditions and diseases and their signs and symptoms the more you will be able to make an educated decision as to whether it is nothing or whether it is something that should be checked by a doctor. The earlier something is detected, the better chance you have of a full recovery.

- Go see a doctor. Most of us have spent at least one sleepless night worrying that some vague symptom was the "Big C." The only way you will stop worrying is to take action and have it checked by a doctor. Most of the time—but not always—it turns out to be nothing and you will walk out of the doctor's office feeling immensely relieved.

If worrying about your health is hurting the quality of life, then by all means, have yourself checked out thoroughly. Often, just knowing your symptoms are not a sign of some dread disease makes the symptoms disappear. Sometimes just a simple change of diet or exercise is the answer. Do everything to assure yourself that you are healthy and then let it go. Stop worrying and go on with your life. And if your symptoms turn out to be something, do what you can to treat that disease or symptom and then focus on something positive.

- Choose not to be a hypochondriac. Some people do create physical ailments because it gets them attention or they are just obsessed with their health. How do you know if you are a hypochondriac or not? If there is really something wrong with your body, it will really let you know. Trust your body. Listen to your body. Get in tune with your body. Real symptoms are not vague. When your body wants you to go to the doctor it will *make sure* you really know it.

I know this for sure because it happened to me, as I mentioned earlier in this book. About five years ago I got up in the morning and urinated. There was blood in my urine. My whole stomach was cramping and I had diarrhea. I knew there was something *really* wrong because my body was yelling at me to get to a doctor. The bottom line is that it turned out to be a rare form of bladder cancer. I am fine now after major cancer surgery, but I can attest to the fact that your body *really* let's you know when it is serious.

- If you are *sure* your symptoms are real, *insist* on being taken seriously. As I mentioned earlier, in 1989 I was sick with fever, dizziness, stiff neck and headache. I dragged from doctor to doctor, but each and every one of them told me that the symptoms were all in my head. One doctor told me I had hypoglycemia and told me to eat hard-boiled eggs and desiccated liver. Another doctor told me I was suffering agoraphobia and I should force myself to go out more.

Finally, I was having what appeared to be a seizure and my husband rushed me to an emergency room. After waiting three hours alone in a room smaller than a jail cell, the doctor came in told me that I was having a panic attack, handed me prescription for Xanax, and told me it was fine to leave on a ski trip to Canada.

I kept on insisting that these symptoms couldn't possibly be in my head. My body was screaming to be helped. It wasn't until I was lying on the bathroom floor half dead and *insisted* on being put in the hospital that a neurologist finally took a spinal tap and determined that I had viral spinal meningitis.

Had I accepted all the doctors' opinions that I was a hypochondriac I probably would have been dead. What I learned from this experience was that we all must be very assertive about our own healthcare. Never take for granted what one particular doctor says is right. Go from doctor to doctor until you are positive that your diagnosis is correct.

- Don't dwell on illness or illness will dwell on you. When you decide you are worthy of happiness, you will want to take all the steps you can to insure that the quality of the rest of your life is good. If you *choose* to be happy, then give up worrying about your health by taking control of your body instead of letting your body control you. Being happy includes feeling well physically as well as mentally.

- Defy your genetics. If you have a family history of heart disease and your cholesterol is 300, it's time to lay off the butter and the spareribs. Do everything in your power to control the conditions that you know you are at high risk for because of your genetics.

Deny Yourself Immediate Gratification

It always amazes me how many seemingly intelligent people I know who are still laying out in the sun because they think they look better with a tan even though they know they are at great risk for melanoma. Or, how many people do you know who order a great big greasy steak when they know that the fat is clogging their arteries and the charred fat from the barbecue is carcinogenic? How many people still smoke and if asked say, "I know it's bad for me. I'll stop soon."

❧ If you want to stop worrying about getting sick stop doing the things that will make you sick. ❧

Stop Worrying About What Everyone Else Thinks

Our culture tells us that we are "supposed to" or "have to" in order to "fit in." Manufacturers promote their products as "must haves" in order to be "cool." Some people spend their entire paycheck on expensive designer clothes and handbags just to impress others. Others have to drive that sporty BMW convertible just to look "successful." One study showed that 25% of the people who are walking around talking on their cell phones to look "important" are not really talking to anybody!

Our self image may not match what we portray to the outside world. When we have low self-esteem we feel we must constantly prove to the outside world that we are okay–"Look at me, I'm good looking, I'm capable, I'm smart, I'm honest, I'm rich. I'm in great shape." But if your happiness is based solely on the image that you have created of yourself in order to convince others that you are okay, then you will never find true happiness. You will always be worried that someone will discover the "real you" underneath the designer duds and sports car.

Rosemary is a beautiful, capable woman, but she is constantly putting herself down. She is always making excuses for how she looks or how her home looks. She tries so hard to be a good wife, a good mother, a good daughter, a good friend, and a good employee that she is plagued by physical symptoms and has even tottered on the edge of a nervous breakdown. It has become so emotionally and physically difficult for Rosemary to keep up her strong image that she is making herself sick. If she doesn't give up this masquerade, her body will force her to.

Coming to terms with your own limitations is necessary in order to achieve happiness. Many very successful people seem to have boundless physical, mental and emotional energy. I can't figure out when they ever sleep. But most of us mere mortals can do only so much before our bodies stop us by getting sick. We all have our own time clock. We all march to the beat of our own drummer. I do believe in making the most of our time on earth and making the most of our days, but many of us try so hard to be superhuman that we end up making ourselves ill.

Our self-esteem is also based on our perceived successes and failures. We think that if we are successful others will shower us with adoration and that if we fail at something others will call us "losers."

If the only reason you seek success is to be admired or adored, then success will not make you happy. The only way to be truly happy is to do something you enjoy. If, in the process, you become successful, that's great. And, if not, you've enjoyed the process.

It is only human nature to want to be adored and admired—if not for one's beauty, then for one's brains, sense of humor, financial success or talents. From the moment we are born we are constantly seeking approval from our parents and our peers. Many people go to their graves feeling unfulfilled, still wishing their mothers or fathers had only said to them "I'm proud of you." Unfortunately, many parents are not psychology-minded enough to say this to their children. If we are still waiting for our parents to tell us how wonderful we are in order to feel good about ourselves, then we might have to wait forever. Give it up.

Reprogram Your Inner Thoughts

If you react strongly to mental stress, chances are you are falling prey to what therapists call "cognitive distortions." These are self-destructive habits that can transform meaningless episodes into anxiety-

producing problems. Identify the following patterns in your own behavior and try to substitute forgiving alternatives:

- All or nothing thinking. You either performed a task perfectly
  or it was a total disaster. You are either incredibly successful or
  you are a total failure. There is no in between. You say to yourself "I didn't get that job, I must be totally incompetent." No
  single episode can define who and what you are. One flaw does
  not make you a flawed person. One mistake does not make you
  a total idiot.

- Discounting the positive. You misinterpret every act of kindness as deception. You find a way to twist a stroke of good luck
  into a stroke of bad luck. You think that every compliment is
  insincere and every success is just a fluke. Compliments are
  more often genuine than not. Accept them graciously. Believe
  that you deserve to have some good luck and success. Believe
  that people genuinely like you and want to make you feel good
  about yourself. The more you believe this the more it becomes
  a self-fulfilling prophecy.

- Assuming the worst. You *know* that things are not going to turn
  out well, that your friends and coworkers are annoyed with you
  and that perfect strangers are making fun of you. You are sure
  that an asteroid is going to hit your new car or a tornado is going to blow your house apart. Force yourself to be optimistic.
  When people's faces and gestures show displeasure, it usually
  isn't about you. They are usually thinking about someone or
  something else. *Choose* to believe that most people are kind
  and nice.

- Over-generalizing. You identify every turn for the worse as part
  of a dark pattern of failure. You think you didn't get that job
  because you *never* get the job. You think that person didn't call
  you back because he or she is rejecting you, like everyone else
  has. You think that all situations are alike. Evaluate each event
  independently because all situations are not the same.

However, if the same thing keeps on happening to you, perhaps you might want to analyze what *did* happen. Did you do or say something that kept you from getting that job or that made that person not want to be with you again? If the answer is "yes," do something about your behavior. If the answer is "no," let it go. It's the other person's problem.

- Personalizing. You assume responsibility for events that are beyond your control. If someone looks at you the wrong way or a friend walks by you without saying "hello" you immediately say to yourself, "What did I do wrong?" The answer is usually *nothing*. If you really did do something wrong, most people will let you know.

❧ *If you* ***choose*** *to have a beautiful life, don't think ugly thoughts.* ❧

Lighten Up

The purpose of life is to be happy and to make others happy. All too often we take what happens to us too seriously. We forget how to find humor in our humanness.

Did you ever notice that some of the worst, most serious situations in your life turn out to be some of the funniest experiences you've ever had when you tell your friends about them later? Wouldn't it be nice if you could see the humor in these traumatic experiences as they are happening to you?

If you *choose* to be happy, *choose* to find humor in even the most difficult of situations. Take yourself outside of your problem, tragedy or dilemma and try to look at it from a different prospective.

Years ago I was watching *Sixty Minutes* and was extremely impressed with Lewis Leakey's son, who had lost both his legs in a plane crash. He laughed about it, saying that, "Being a double amputee is a plus because when I travel and everyone else's legs are pushed up against the seat in front of them, I just take off my legs and lean back." Here is a man who could find humor in his tragedy—a happy man who could have just as easily become bitter.

Smile

A smile attracts people to you like a magnet. If you are happy, you smile a lot. People are drawn to you because your smile makes them feel good about themselves. They smile back, which, in turn, makes you feel good about yourself. It has been scientifically proven that the physical act of smiling will create positive feelings. So if you want to feel better just smile and you will automatically feel better. *Try it now!*

When I was married to my first husband my self-esteem was so low that I would wander around all day going in and out of stores. When a salesperson spoke to me I didn't have the confidence to say anything back. I felt intimidated by everyone. I felt so awful about myself that I mumbled and could barely form a complete sentence because I didn't believe that what I was saying was important. I would get comments from strangers like "Oh, come on, life isn't that bad, is it?" I would feign an obligatory smile and then retreat into my own self-inflicted misery.

When something good happened and I wanted to be happy, I couldn't act cheerful because it felt uncomfortable. I was actually more comfortable being miserable.

I always felt that I was on the outside looking in—alienated from mainstream society. That everyone else belonged and I didn't. That everyone else was in an inner circle of people and I was an outcast. I was deeply unhappy.

One day I woke up as if out of a 10-year coma and decided that I deserved to be happy. That happiness was my *choice*. So, by leaving my marriage, reaching out to make new friends, getting a job, reading every self-help book on the market, and realizing that my feelings of alienation from others was unfounded, I was able to gain the confidence I needed to start my life anew. And I began to smile again.

I have been going to the same health club three or four times a week for many years. There is a new instructor. He has only been there six months but he's about the most popular person I've ever met. I've been taking his step and kickboxing classes and have finally realized what it is that makes Heinz so well liked. He is always smiling. He is always happy. He is charismatic. He has a wonderful sense of humor. He knows how to make every one of his students feel special. Heinz has a way of making me smile no matter how bad a day I've had.

er is contagious and when you laugh along with them you feel happy

happy. Laughter can make your problems seem lighter as well as boost your immune system. Laughter is *essential* to happiness.

Some people seem to be so uptight that they are afraid to let go and laugh. A friend of my husband who is a comedian and magician was performing a few weeks ago. There were three single women sitting at a table together who all looked disappointed at the lack of single men they had apparently come to meet. When the magician asked them to participate, they had these looks on their faces like "I dare you to make me laugh." No matter what he said or did to make them laugh, they had this defiant "You can't make me laugh" look on their faces. Are you one of those people who defy everyone and everything to make you happy? Do you watch a comedy show and defy the comedian to make you laugh? If so, you are sabotaging your own happiness.

See Life as a Gift

Our lives are miniscule in relationship to the size and time frame of the Universe. Life has gone on millions of years before us and it probably will go on millions of years after we're gone, so why not just enjoy the gift we have been given and enjoy life *now*?

Do we have to know the reason and motive behind a gift to enjoy a gift? Should we not enjoy a gift because someone might take it away from us someday? Or because we are not sure how it was made or who made it? Or because a few little pieces are missing? Or because someone else next to us got a better gift?

Don't Take Life So Seriously

When I asked my always-happy 105-year-old father-in-law what the secret of his happiness was, he replied, "I just don't take anything too seriously." It was such a simple philosophy and yet so true.

Chapter 15

Be Your Authentic Self

Love Yourself

In order to be at peace with yourself, it's important to be 100% honest about yourself to yourself and others. You should never have to feel embarrassed by your physical appearance, your behavior, or your failures. You should never have to feel ashamed of anything that you've done in your past or that you have to hide anything from anyone or pretend that you are someone or something that you are not. You cannot be a fraud and be happy. It is impossible. If you *choose* to be happy, you must accept that nothing or no one is perfect, even you, and that no one worth having in your life expects you to be.

Learn to love yourself by being the best *you* you can be. If you are always your *authentic self*, you will be happier. It is so much easier to be your authentic self than it is to present yourself to the world in a way that is not who you really are.

Some people think that they would be happy if only they could find soul mates to love them. Others think that they would be happy if only their parents would love them more. Still others think that they would be happy if they had more friends who loved them. But the truth is that these people would be happy if they just learned to love themselves.

Barbra Streisand, interviewed on *Sixty Minutes* many years ago, was practically reduced to tears when she shared with the audience how hurt she was that her mother had refused to tell her that she was proud of her. Here was this incredibly talented and successful woman who had achieved fame and fortune of the utmost magnitude and she was still worried about what her mother thought of her. She still needed parental approval.

Hopefully by now you realize that if your inner thoughts are loving thoughts that you should love yourself in spite of what *anyone* thinks, including your parents. You don't need to prove anything to *anyone*.

And if you truly love yourself, everyone, including your parents, will love you instinctively.

If you want to be loved, just think loving thoughts.

Stop Making Every Problem into a Catastrophe

Everything that happens to you in your life is not a major disaster. When your car gets towed away or your hairdresser burns off all your hair, remind yourself that years from now you will be laughing about this incident. Always find humor in every situation. Say to yourself, "This, too, shall pass." Save the dramatics for the real tragedies, which, hopefully, are few and far between.

But sometimes life does throw you a curve ball. What if a real catastrophe has happened to you recently? Perhaps you lost your mate, your child, a parent, your home, your job, your business, you were diagnosed with a terminal illness, or you were in a debilitating accident. There are stages of mourning loss that most people go through and there are many books that will help you get through this period. However, knowing the stages of mourning and going through them will not make you emerge happy. The only way to be happy is to work at being happy, and, if you are genetically unhappy, you will have to work twice as hard.

Remember my "Fifteen Percent Principle." You can bet on the fact that you will not get through life without going through at least some catastrophes, life crises or traumas. As a matter of fact, you may estimate that at least 15% of your life will be spent dealing with your own catastrophes, life crises or traumas or those of the people to whom you are close.

The first thing to say when something horrible happens is, "Aha, this is one of those obligatory misfortunes that are included in my 15% share of disasters I must endure." This type of thinking will answer the question you are bound to ask, which is, "Why me, God?" The answer is that it is just part of the 15% obligatory crises you must endure. Remind yourself that soon you will be able to enjoy the remaining 85% non-crises period of your life.

∾ *The **secret** is to maintain a positive attitude and a sense of humor no matter what happens to you.* ∾

Elizabeth just taught me a very valuable lesson about how to stay happy even while you are going through part of your 15% share of your life's crises. As I told you about in the first chapter, Elizabeth is one of those people who was born happy. When she moved to San Francisco she used to get in the car alone and drive down to Los Angeles. It took her at least six or seven hours. She said she loved it. She just turned on some old Frank Sinatra tapes and sang along and had a wonderful time.

Now I, being a genetically unhappy person, was driving in the car and I was playing a tape of old Bobby Vinton songs. I love the song Blue Velvet, so I decided to sing along with it. But I couldn't do it. So I decided to force myself. I felt silly, but I did it anyway. It wasn't long before I was singing louder and louder and really enjoying myself. I realized that forcing yourself to learn to sing along in the car is a wonderful exercise in letting go and being happy. Force yourself to be happy even if you are not. If you fake a feeling long enough you will eventually actually feel that feeling. Trick yourself into being happy.

You Can't Get Through Life Problem Free

Everyone gets his or her share of poop. But why do some people seem to have hard, crises-filled lives and other people seem to sail through life? Perhaps it's just karma. Perhaps it's just the luck of the draw. Perhaps it's their positive or negative attitude about life.

When something bad happens to you, think of it as when your credit card bill arrives. Now you have to pay for all the things you've been enjoying. Crises can happen early in life. Think of this as prepaying your bill, kind of like a bank debit card. Crises can happen in midlife. Think of this as the pay-as-you-go plan. When crises happen in later life, think of yourself as lucky for having lived on interest-free money for so long.

If this theory doesn't work for you, try this one. Think of the crises in your life as the dues that you have to pay for belonging to an exclusive club called Life. In joining this club you get unlimited privileges to enjoy the wonders of Mother Nature, to laugh and have a good time, to meet new friends, to travel, to do basically anything you enjoy. In return, you must pay a "Fifteen Percent Crisis Dues" in order to keep up your membership. Keep in mind, this is a lifetime membership. Once you join, you can't quit the club until you die. So pay your dues gracefully, endure your crises as required, and enjoy the 85% fun time of your membership.

Learn From Your Mistakes

Fifteen percent of everything you do, think and say in life is going to be a mistake. The only way not to make mistakes is to not do, think or say anything. Vegetables do not make mistakes. People do.

Life is constantly sending you messages. Pay attention to them. Use your mistakes as learning processes. Ask yourself what you did to create a specific negative situation. If you *choose* to be happy, don't repeat that mistake. The next time you have the same situation, remind yourself of what you did wrong the last time.

If there is something about your behavior that you suspect is creating negative results, find out what mistakes you are making. Ask your friends, family and coworkers to be honest about what they think you are doing wrong. Accept their constructive criticism gracefully. Try as hard as you can to change the behavior that is creating negative results.

Unhappy, negative people get defensive if you tell them what they did or are doing wrong because they need more fuel in order to remain unhappy and negative. They defend and make excuses for their actions. They don't want to know if they are making mistakes and thus, don't have any intention of learning from their mistakes.

Happy, positive people couldn't care less if they did or said something wrong. They know that they are not perfect and don't pretend to be. They know that if they do and say enough things in life they are bound to make mistakes. They see their mistakes as positive learning experiences.

❧ *Happy, positive people **learn** from their mistakes.* ❧

Be Patient

Accept that most everything you try to accomplish will take at least 15% longer than you had estimated it would take. If you accept this fact, you will live 15% longer.

Everything in life has a natural flow to it and happens in its own good time. If you have to rush anything, you will probably end up regretting it. If what you want to happen hasn't happened yet, your Higher Spirit usually has a good reason. Once you accept this reality, you can relax and good things will slowly start to happen for you.

Did you ever notice when you are rushed you get anxious and nervous? You tend to be clumsy and make a lot of mistakes. This is a sign that you are doing too much and pushing too hard. Learn to relax. Ask yourself, "What is the worst thing that can happen if this doesn't get done?"

Did you ever notice that celebrities that rise too fast get into trouble? Like John Beluchi, River Phoenix or Elvis Presley? Life happens too fast for them. They resort to caffeine, alcohol and drugs in order to keep up the hectic pace and then use downers in order to get some rest because they have so much anxiety.

Everyone has his or her own natural pace. Some people are in slow motion. They talk slowly, they move slowly. It takes them forever to make one simple decision. If your pace is too slow, it may be a sign of depression. Depressed people are often very sluggish and it takes them a lot of effort to do anything.

Others are always in a hurry, but you can never figure out where they are going. If your pace is too high-speed, maybe you are running so fast and doing so much because you are afraid of what you'll find if you slow down and have to spend time with yourself. Fast paced people are rarely alone. They need others to validate their self-worth.

> ❧ *It is impossible to find true happiness if you can't sit still long enough to look inside yourself for it.* ❧

Hopefully, your pace is somewhere in between. But, no matter what your pace, try to live your life at a speed that is comfortable for you. To speed things up is to create anxiety and unhappiness. To slow things down is to create boredom.

Be Optimistic

If you think nothing good will ever happen to you, nothing good will ever happen to you. If you think an idea of yours will never work, it will never work. If you think you won't get the job, the mate or the money, you won't. Remember, your thoughts are self-fulfilling prophecies. Negative things happen to negative people. Positive things happen to positive people.

I was brought up to be a negative person. If I wanted to spend some money, my mother would say, "You're going to put us in the poor house." As a child, I actually thought if we spent too much money that our whole family was going to be locked up in some institution called "The Poor House." If I asked my father for anything, he said to me "You're going to give me an ulcer." Until adulthood I walked around thinking that I was responsible for my father's dying of cancer because I nagged him for an angora sweater when I was 13 years old.

So, how do you exorcise the negative demons that haunt you? Assuming your pessimism is 50% genetic and 50% environmental from your childhood, the only way to get rid of your glumness is to work 24 hours a day fighting your gloom. When a negative thought enters your mind, acknowledge it to yourself or even out loud to someone who understands—then rephrase your thought to be positive. Do this every time a negative thought enters your mind. Eventually, if you refuse to let negative thoughts invade your mind, they will stop coming little by little, kind of like unwanted houseguests when you stop feeding them. You don't go from being a negative person to a positive person overnight any more than you become a concert pianist overnight. It takes years and years of practice.

~ *The only reward for being a pessimist is that you have an extremely good chance that you will be right.* ~

Declare Yourself to Be a Lucky Person

Why do some people seem luckier than others? It's because lucky people always have a positive attitude about what will happen to them. If you see yourself as a lucky person then you *are* a lucky person and good things will happen to you. And when bad things happen to you, you are still a lucky person who has just had something unfortunate happen to you.

Let's take one example and show the difference between a happy person's attitude and an unhappy person's attitude. Suppose you had a car accident. Your brand new car is a wreck and your neck is a little sore and you missed a big important meeting. The unhappy person thinks of himself as unlucky because he was in an accident. The positive, happy person will see himself as lucky because he didn't die. Which one are you?

Make Your Own Good Luck

- Count your blessings. Appreciate the good luck you *do* have. You are not a starving child in Africa or a corpse floating down the river in India. Sure, right, you say, that really isn't much consolation when I can't even pay my bills or feel so lonely that I want to die. This type of thinking will never make you happy. If you don't count your little blessings why should you be blessed with bigger blessings? If you were your Higher Spirit, would you keep on giving bigger and bigger gifts to someone who doesn't even appreciate a small gift?

  ∾ *If you want larger blessings, you must first be grateful for the smaller blessings you already have.* ∾

- Always think of yourself as a lucky person. Never use negative words like, "With my luck I'll never find a parking space." Instead, substitute words like, "I have a parking fairy so I'm sure I will get a good parking space." Create your own positive reality by throwing out a positive energy force into the Universe.

- Get rid of all the negative influences in your life now. Surround yourself with positive, lucky people.

- Think only positive thoughts.

- Take only positive actions.

- Speak only positive words.

- Whenever something that appears unlucky happens, twist it around so that it can be construed as lucky. For instance, recently my husband and I had come home and the upstairs neighbor's washing machine hose had broken and completely flooded our condo. What a mess. However, it completely ruined our 20-year-old sofas. I twisted the whole episode around to show *how lucky* we were because the insurance company paid for us to buy two brand new sofas.

❧ *When God gives you lemons, make lemonade.* ❧

Jody always sees herself as a lucky person. Whenever something happens to her, she says, "See, that's because I'm a lucky person." She is a lucky person because she perceives herself that way.

Ten years ago Jody was diagnosed with a low-grade form of leukemia. She has chosen to take the holistic approach and has not given in to conventional medicine yet. She has a wonderful quality of life and feels great. Yes, her white blood count is going down, but she doesn't seem to worry. She never complains. If you ask her she will tell you that her neck is swollen and she doesn't like how it looks, but that she is not uncomfortable.

On the other hand, Larry was diagnosed with the same form of leukemia about six months before Jody. He had a different attitude. He used his illness as an attention-getting device. He took the conventional route, enjoying the drama and attention of his family and friends and the doctors and nurses. After much pain and suffering, he died about eight years ago.

No one is lucky 100% of the time, but no one is unlucky 100% of the time either. A gambler can't win 24 hours a day, day in and day out, no matter how skilled and how lucky he is. But, it is statistically impossible to work and work and try and try and not have at least a few successes. If you are a gambler you already know that every time you roll the dice you have the exact same odds of rolling any particular number that you had on any previous roll or have on any future roll.

Accept that most of the time you are a lucky person, but some of the time your luck isn't quite as good. When things don't work out the way you would have wanted them to, think of it as a learning experience. A positive person turns the things that didn't work out well into blessings in disguise.

Thank your Higher Spirit for all the lucky things that happen to you. Your Higher Spirit likes to be appreciated and will reward you with more lucky things if you acknowledge the good it has done for you.

How to Change Your Luck

Naomi and Ethel are a gay couple who used to live in Los Angeles. They were having financial problems. Naomi had written some screenplays and Ethel was a photographer. In Los Angeles they were tiny fish in a big ocean, so they moved to North Carolina where they were big fish in a little lake. Now they have started their own successful photography, screenwriting, and acting school. They were brave enough to throw in their cards and, with much optimism, draw a new, winning hand.

If you've tried everything and nothing is working, maybe you should try something completely different. It just might work!

Psychologist Matthew Smith, who conducts research at England's University of Hertfordshire, along with fellow researchers Richard Wiseman and Peter Harris, believes that luck has more to do with how each of us sees the world rather than how the world sees fit to treat us. In a pilot study, Smith asked 100 self-described lucky and unlucky subjects to flip a coin 20 times and predict the outcome. The subjects who considered themselves "lucky" guessed their accuracy correctly, while the "unlucky" subjects underestimated their success. Smith says, "Whether people consider themselves lucky or unlucky, they tend to remember events in a way that supports their convictions."

Chip Denman, manager of the University of Maryland's statistics lab and a founder of National Capital Area Skeptics, says, "People see patterns where none actually exist. For example, luck—good or bad—comes in threes." He believes that your perception of luck is directly related to your knowledge of probability. For instance, what are the chances that if you have 23 people in the same room, at least two of them will share the same birthday? Most people guess about one in 150. The actual answer is one in two. The "lucky people" see amazing good fortune in things that are actually quite likely to happen.

If you consider yourself unlucky and think that everything in your life is going to turn out for the worst, you will be reluctant to take chances, such as invest in the stock market. If you realize that you have some control over your fate, you may take the chances and reap the rewards (or accept the losses.)

The most important thing is to learn from your luck. If you are unlucky in love, for example, and keep finding yourself with unacceptable partners, stand back and take a good look at what you are doing to attract unsuitable types instead of just thinking that you are unlucky in love.

Proclaim Yourself a Winner

You are what you think you are. If you think you are a loser, you are a loser. If you think you are a winner, you are a winner. What you put out is what you get back. If you put out the negative energy of a loser, you will lose. If you put out the positive energy of a winner, you will win.

Please don't confuse this with being phony. There is nothing more obnoxious than a real estate agent telling you he's had his best year yet when you know the real estate market has been dead because of the recession and there hasn't been a sale in the area for the past two years. It is very nice to keep up one's self image for personal as well as business reasons, but out and out lying is deception.

If you *choose* to be happy you must be honest with yourself and others. So, what do you do if you want to put out positive "winner" energy and yet nothing you have done lately has been indicative that you actually are a positive "winner"?

No one wants a real estate agent that is desperate for a deal anymore than anyone wants a mate who is desperate for love. You must find your own way of exuding confidence without being phony and deceptive. Others will have more confidence in you and more respect for you if you are honest. You will have more respect for yourself if you are honest. Try to be truthful without being desperate.

*❧ You **are** a winner 100% of the time. It is just that some of the time you don't get winning results. The best racehorse still loses a few races. ❧*

Live in the Moment

The past is gone and there is nothing you can do to change it. Don't beat yourself up for the mistakes that you have already made. You made the best decisions you knew how to make based on what you knew at the time. If the decisions didn't turn out right, it's not your fault. Remind yourself that it's not that you made a bad decision, but rather that you made a good decision that turned out bad.

The future is the unknown. It's the reason we get out of bed in the morning. It's the reason we keep on turning the pages of a good novel. We want to find out what happens next. However, to live your life based on what is going to be in the future is to not enjoy the here and now. When you read a good novel, it is the hours of turning the pages in suspense that gives you the most amount of pleasure rather than just the few minutes when you find out the ending.

❧ If you don't enjoy the process, winning is meaningless. ❧

Stop Being So Critical

Are you too critical? Do you always find something wrong with everyone and everything? When you find yourself criticizing another person, ask yourself if it is really that same quality in yourself that you are criticizing. If you are trying to figure out what it is that is making you unhappy, the first place to look is at what you don't like about other people. You are the most critical of the flaws in others that most remind you of your own flaws.

People don't like to be criticized because it is a direct assault on their self image. Protecting one's self image is everyone's first priority. Therefore, if you criticize someone (including yourself) you are opening yourself up wide for conflict. Conflict will bring you unhappiness.

For instance, let's say you have a little problem like my friend Adrianna does. When her husband, Mike, does the dishes he puts the spoons together with the handles facing up in the dishwasher. Her dishwasher is not the newest or most expensive model and so it does not clean spoons that have been loaded in this manner.

She has asked Mike many times, "Honey, can you please put the spoons face up in the dishwasher because they never get clean and I have to put them through the dishwasher again."

He replies, "You always criticize everything I do!"

Adrianna says, "This is not an assault on everything you do, it's only a request that you load the spoons face up in the dishwasher."

Mike storms out of the room screaming, "You don't think I can do anything right!"

This, of course, escalates into three days of not talking to Adrianna except for scolding her for not treating him right. This drains her of all of her energy and all she wants to do is sleep.

First, Adrianna should count her blessings—she has a wonderful husband who washes the dishes in spite of the fact that he puts the spoons in wrong. If Adrianna *chooses* to be happy, she should keep quiet and hope that someday when he is unloading the dishwasher he will notice that the spoons are all stuck together with disgusting goop and that it will occur to him to load the spoons correctly.

If you *choose* to be happy, choose not to criticize anyone unnecessarily. It will ultimately make *you* unhappy and strain your relationship with that person. But, if you must criticize someone, make sure you pick a time when that person is in a good mood. Remember, *timing is everything*. Begin by reinforcing that person's self image by telling him or her all the wonderful things that he or she does correctly. Then, let him or her know something you have done wrong so that you humanize yourself. Make the behavior you are criticizing about him or her the least important aspect of the conversation.

Another method to avoid making the object of your criticism defensive is the indirect approach. Let's say you have a friend who always interrupts a conversation and never lets you finish your sentence. Instead of actually criticizing this person for interrupting, tell this person a story about a problem you have with "another friend" who is always interrupting. Hopefully, your friend will realize that he or she is guilty of the same behavior and do something about it and never realize that you were criticizing him or her.

Don't make fun of people who don't live up to your standards of beauty. Remember that you get back what you put out. Be compassionate. Not everyone is beautiful or handsome in a conventional way. Look for something good about every person. Perhaps it's a smile or a twinkle in his or her eyes. If he or she looks sad, have compassion for his or her sadness.

Recently I showed a group of friends, including Elizabeth, a photograph I had taken at a party of a woman. One of the women in the photograph was very heavy and very homely, and that's a compliment. Elizabeth studied the picture for a moment and then declared, "She has great eyebrows!"

> ∾ *One of the most important secrets of happiness is to find something positive about everyone and everything.* ∾

Whenever I find myself thinking critical thoughts about someone, I tell myself that my punishment will be coming back in my next life as that person.

If Someone Criticizes You

- You are usually wrong if you think, "If they are criticizing me they must dislike me."

- Don't react with a temper tantrum because it will only trigger a dangerous silence. Instead, just accept the criticism graciously.

- Listen to it instead of focusing on the critic. A person must really care about you if he or she takes the time to criticize you. Maybe his or her criticism is valid.

- Listen to everything the criticizer is saying and make sure you understand it. Evaluate whether this is something you want to change or not. And consider the source. Evaluate the competency of the critic.

- Say thank you.

If You Must Criticize Someone

- Never criticize what cannot be changed, such as, "You shouldn't have worn that shirt tonight." This kind of criticism can only hurt the person and make him or her feel uncomfortable all night.
- Choose the right time and place. Don't criticize someone in front of others.
- Don't criticize when you are in an angry mood. You will only say something you wish you hadn't.
- Start with a positive remark. Tell the other person something good about himself or herself or what he or she has done.
- Be specific. State exactly what is wrong.
- Praise improvement.

Learn to Trust Again

Just because you have been deceived and hurt before in your life doesn't mean that everyone is deceptive and will hurt you. If you live your life trying to protect yourself from hurt, you will never experience the true pleasures of relationships. To live is to risk being hurt emotionally and physically. To be happy you must learn to forgive the person or event that hurt you and move on.

Be the Kind of Person You Would Like to Have as a Friend

In order to be liked by other people you have to genuinely like yourself. In order to like yourself you have to be a good person, the kind of person that you would choose to be your best friend. People are intuitive. They know when you are thinking honest and good thoughts and they know when you are thinking mean and evil thoughts.

If you are not really thinking loving thoughts, then you are not being loving. And if you are not a loving person to others, you probably don't love yourself. And if you don't love yourself, how can you expect anyone else to love you?

❧ *In order to be loved, you **must be** loving. Mother Teresa once said, "Being loved by no one is the worst disease."*❧

What You See in the Mirror is What You Are

Your physical appearance is a reflection of how you feel inside. If you feel unhappy, you will dress slovenly and carry yourself with a slouch. If you feel happy, you will dress neatly and have good posture. Creating a more confident outward appearance will make people respond more positively to you and open up more opportunities in your social and love life as well as your career. In return, you will be happier.

Lori lives a chaotic life. Her house is a mess, her career is a mess, her social life is a mess, and she can't seem to get her life together. Her mind is in chaos. At 48 years old, she doesn't have a specific goal. She gets sidetracked. She loses track of time. She loses everything. She leaves her purse on the top the car and drives off. She loses important checks that she was supposed to mail. The only way Lori is going to get her life in order is to get her mind in order first.

Ingrid is always wearing torn clothes pulled together with safety pins and shoes with the heels worn down. Her purse is filled with unpaid bills and old candy wrappers. Her car is one big scrape and ding. At home, there are old food wrappers in bathroom drawers. Ingrid floats from job to job, apartment to apartment, friend to friend. How can she find inner peace and happiness when her life is constantly coming apart at the seams?

Angela rented a space in an antique mall. She would run around the city to garage sales and thrift shops and find bargains that she could sell at a profit. One day she called me in a panic. She was totally overwhelmed with work. She asked me if I could come over and help her organize all the items that she wanted to display in her space. When I arrived at the antique mall, she was sitting on the floor, crying, surrounded by boxes and boxes of merchandise.

I asked, "How did you accumulate so much stuff?"

She said, "I've been buying for months and putting everything in my garage."

I asked, "How often do you come by your space in the antique mall?"

"Oh," she said, "I haven't bothered coming here in two months."

If you don't keep up your chores on a daily basis, eventually they will pile up and become overwhelming. Had Angela organized her work day so that she spent part of it looking for items to sell and part of it unpacking and pricing the merchandise in her space at the antique mall, this crisis would never have happened.

Happy people lead calm, organized lives. They create systems and schedules that allow them to get everything done that they need to do without creating undo stress. They usually look impeccable and their homes and cars are perfectly neat and clean. This is because they are mentally healthy and *choose* not to create more stress for themselves than life offers naturally.

Get Organized

It's hard to be happy if you are always stressed out about having too much to do and not enough time to do it in. Create an organized system of managing your tasks, errands and calls each day instead of letting them pile up and become unmanageable and stressful. Organize your tasks, errands and phone calls on separate lists. Prioritize these three lists so that the most important tasks, errands and calls are done first. Reorganize, update and reprioritize these lists weekly. This approach eliminates stress. You can't find inner peace and happiness if your life is in total chaos.

Clean up your mind as if you were cleaning out your garage of useless clutter. If your thoughts are scattered, your life will be scattered, too. Organize your thoughts by answering the following questions:

- What are my short-term goals?

- What are my long-term goals?

- What are my responsibilities?

- What people do not live up to my standards and do not add anything positive to my life?

- What responsibilities do I have that are not necessary and that only complicate my life?

- What possessions do I have that are no longer useful and are just collecting dust?

Then, eliminate the responsibilities, possessions and people that are cluttering your thoughts and your life.

Stop Being So Self Absorbed

Are you the center of the Universe? Do you spend all your time and energy focusing so much on yourself that you have no energy left to listen to anyone else? Focusing only on yourself will make you unhappy. Focusing on other people or interests outside of yourself will make you happy. The happiest people of all are those that spend time helping others and giving back to society.

If you *choose* to be happy, embrace the truth—the whole world *does not* revolve around *you*. Life is not about *you*. Most everyone is interested in his or her own welfare. Nobody wants to be constantly bothered by your problems and dilemmas. To dwell on yourself and your unhappiness is to attract more unhappiness. Try to sense what other people are thinking and feeling instead of fixating on your own life. Do something nice for a friend, a stranger or mankind. Remember, like attracts like.

Kelly is so self-absorbed that she is totally disinterested in anyone or anything that doesn't have anything to do with her own self-gratification. She talks incessantly about herself. If you try to interject a word or two, she talks right through you. She is too busy focusing on herself to even notice that you want to say something. She never asks about you or anyone else unless it is on a phone machine when she won't have to bother to listen to the answer. Time spent with Kelly is frustrating and exhausting. She wonders why she just cannot find someone to marry and with whom to have children, but she won't shut up long enough for you to give her the answer. The irony is that Kelly complains about all the men she goes out with. "All they want to do is talk about themselves," she gripes. Is this not proof positive that the traits we don't like in other people are usually the traits people don't like about us?

You will find happiness when you stop dwelling on yourself and start focusing on the needs of other people. Become a good listener. Unhappy people are not usually good listeners. They are too busy worrying about what they are going to say next about themselves to listen to what you have to say. They turn everything someone else says into something that has to do with them. It is much more rewarding to just listen to what the other person is saying and respond accordingly only when he or she has finished.

People will care more about you if you care about them. Buy a daily planner with an address book and a daily calendar. Write down all appointments, addresses, phone numbers, fax numbers, birthdays, children's names, pets' names, parents' names and so on. Take notes when you're on the telephone. Write down information people give you—their vacations, their doctor appointments, their job interviews, their dates—anything that will remind you to call and ask them how things went. They will be pleased you remembered and you will feel happy that you made them feel important.

Develop Social Graces

Needless to say, talking with your mouth full will not gain you popularity. Be on your best behavior, but don't be so unnatural that you become uptight and guarded. Let other people see your flaws. It will make them feel more comfortable about their own flaws and like you even more.

Strive to make others feel good about themselves. It should make you happy when you make someone else feel good. Most people are suffering from the same or worse self-esteem issues as you are. You will find people will light up when you compliment them. *Be a happiness giver!*

Don't Let Others Make You Feel Guilty for Being Happy

The other night I walked into the health club excited because I had just finished making reservations for a trip to New York. I was going to see my long lost aunt and cousins as well as go to a few plays, trendy restaurants, and some museums.

I ran into Francine and told her. She looked at me judgmentally and said, "Oh? New York? Business or pleasure?"

I said, "Pleasure."

"Oh, well, you'll have a good time," she said with a tone mixed with jealousy and how dare I spend my money that way and enjoy myself.

I walked away feeling guilty for planning a fun and exciting vacation.

If you *choose* to be happy, wish good things to happen to you, but also wish good things to happen to everyone—and avoid jealous people like the plague. They are *toxic* with a capital "T."

Change Your Patterns

If something isn't working, try something else. Keep on trying different things until something finally works. If nothing you try ever works out right, ask your friends if they can see what it is you are doing that is creating negative results. Usually other people can see what you are doing wrong better than you can see it yourself.

Try to find the underlying reasons why bad things keep on happening to you. For instance, if you are accident prone, perhaps you are nervous because you have too many things on your mind and can't concentrate on your driving. If you are always sick, maybe you are under too much stress, which weakens your immune system. Reduce your stress by getting more organized, listening to relaxing music, and taking yoga classes.

If you are always broke perhaps you are living beyond your means. Or perhaps you have a "broke mentality." You find a way to spend every cent you have the minute you get it. Try to make a budget and stick to it. Write down everything you spend on that isn't necessary and stop spending on those things.

If you are always being fired, perhaps there is something you are doing to irritate coworkers or bosses. Ask them what you are doing. People are usually very kind when you ask them for constructive criticism.

Diane is always getting fired. She goes from one job to another. She is always jubilant when she tells you about her latest job, but once she's on the job a few days she decides that she is going to run the office. She takes over. Her flamboyant personality is boisterous and disruptive to the other workers. If she makes a mistake she cries or shouts. Needless to say, this gets on everyone's nerves. Then Diane gets fired again. It's always someone else's fault. The boss is a very "sick" man. The other secretaries were "jealous" of her. Diane is now out of work and very unhappy again. This is a pattern. You would think Diane would ask her friends, "What am I doing wrong?" But she doesn't. If anyone tries to suggest that it could possibly be her fault, she snaps at them. It is never her fault. In Diane's mind she is always right and no one is going to tell her differently. Diane will never find success and happiness until she's willing to see what she is doing to create her own negative patterns.

Vicky finds men who are losers and more than thrilled to be with someone as attractive as she. She has a million neuroses and fears that these men cater to. In the long run, each of these men finally realize how weak and needy Vicky really is and end up taking out their frustrations about being a loser on her. Vicky becomes the victim again. A role she is comfortable with.

Beth finds men who are saviors. She is cute, fun to be with, and has a good sense of humor, but she hasn't learned to give people their space. She was engaged to Mark, a good-looking successful man. She moved in with him. He started having business problems. Instead of being helpful and understanding, she became more and more demanding of his time and energy. He asked her to move out. She refused. He threatened her. Now she became the victim, a role she was comfortable with, too. It's always the other person's fault. It's never her fault. She has never learned from her experiences nor asked anyone what it is that she could be doing wrong.

How does the job-after-job pattern relate to the man-after-man pattern? In both cases, the person refuses to see what it is she is doing to create the unwanted results. Until you see what you are doing to sabotage your own life, you will keep on getting negative results. In order to break an unsuccessful pattern, you must be willing to change that behavior.

*Life changes for you when **you** change.*

Patricia was a beautiful girl who desperately wanted to live the opulent lifestyle of the rich and famous that she read about in movie magazines while she was growing up. She developed expensive taste and always tried to look and act as if she were a rich celebrity. She changed her name to something more glamorous and got a job as a flight attendant, her ticket out of the Midwest.

Tempted by the glitz of Hollywood and Beverly Hills in the mid-seventies, she quit her job as a flight attendant and moved to Hollywood so she could concentrate on finding a rich husband to provide her with the lavish lifestyle she desired. Unfortunately, there were no men looking for women who wanted free rides—because *there are no free rides*. There is a price to pay for everything. She was able to change her appearance with multiple plastic surgeries and her name with one legal document, but she was unable to change her way of thinking.

She attracted losers, liars and con men that would promise her the world, sleep with her, and dump her. No matter what grandiose story they told her about their net worth, she believed them.

Finally, Patricia decided she would make her fortune without a man. She went to every pyramid party and fell for every multi-level marketing sales pitch. She tried every get-rich scheme there was. But once again, Patricia was broke and so desperate to be taken care of that she would hook up with anyone who would provide her with a roof over her head.

Patricia is now a middle-aged woman who is stuck in an abusive relationship. She has become a prisoner. This man will not allow her to go out without him. She has no friends. She lives her life trying to make him happy so that he won't get mad at her and fly into a rage. She says she wants to get away from this man, but there is always an excuse why she cannot leave.

Patricia has not learned one of life's most important lessons: *Be your authentic self.*

*❧ If you try to become someone you are not,
you will meet with failure. If you try to be the best
you you can be, you will meet with success. ❧*

Get Real

Happy people feel comfortable inside their own skin. They don't feel a need to impress others with their great wealth, beauty or intelligence. What you see is what you get.

There are the plastic surgery junkies who never feel young enough or pretty or handsome enough. They are obsessed with their looks and aging and are always trying to recreate themselves, thinking that each new surgery will make them happier. *It won't.*

There are the pathological liars who never feel as if they are interesting enough. They think that if they make up elaborate stories they will appear more important. The end result is that the liar is always found out, and no one wants to be with someone whom they can't believe.

Some people have such low self-esteem that they can never be alone. They spend their life surrounding themselves with "friends" who adore them and tell them that they are wonderful. Their feelings of self-worth come from the adoration they get from other people.

Some people are obsessed with money. They must have the biggest and the best houses, diamond rings and cars. Each expensive possession erroneously proves to them that they are worthwhile.

If you *choose* to be happy, you must accept your humanness and your flaws. Sometimes you get a pimple on the tip of your nose. Sometimes you say the wrong things. Sometimes you forget things or make mistakes. Sometimes you just don't look your best. *It's okay.*

Many people are insecure and often feel like imposters. They have learned to say and do the things that make them socially acceptable, but they really don't feel comfortable with who they are or what they've become. Some people don't even like themselves and are always trying to cover up their inner thoughts.

So, who is the real you? Are you smiling on the outside and dying of emotional pain on the inside? Are you pretending that you are successful when inside you are feeling like a loser? In order to be *real*, you must get in touch with what you are *really* feeling. Other people are smarter than you think. They can sense that you are covering up other feelings. It makes them uneasy because they don't feel as if they are really getting through to you.

The real paradox here is that you can't walk around complaining to your friends and strangers about how miserable you are or how you feel like a failure. That makes you a toxic person, so you have learned to cover up your feelings so that people will accept you.

So what's a person to do? Work on the problem. Find a happy medium. If you are feeling unsuccessful, don't walk around over-compensating by bragging about how much money you are making. You are only making an idiot out of yourself. And if you are feeling alone, don't walk around telling people how busy you are and how many parties you've been invited to because you are being a phony.

To be *real*, focus outside of yourself. Guide conversations to subjects beyond yourself. Don't always dwell on your problems, just work on them privately.

Overcome Your Feelings of Rejection

Do you set yourself up for rejection? Do you expect others to let you down or leave you? Do you leave people before they can leave you?

Remember, you get back from life exactly what you *expect* you will get back.

You didn't get the job you really wanted. You are madly in love with last night's date but he or she won't return your phone call. Your mate just left you for someone 20 years younger. Your friends all had a party and didn't invite you.

First, accept that you cannot please all of the people all of the time. There is always another job, another date, another mate or another friend. Don't drive yourself crazy trying to figure out what you did wrong. Stop tormenting yourself. It's possible you did nothing wrong. Maybe you didn't get the job because someone twice as qualified came in after you and accepted the job for half the salary. Maybe last night's date won't return the phone call because the chemistry just isn't right and he or she does not have the courage to tell you. Maybe your mate left you because they are going through mid-life crisis. If your husband runs off with his young, beautiful secretary it does not mean that you are unattractive, not sexy, or unworthy—it just means that your husband cannot be trusted. Cheating on you is not very nice. Who wants a mate like that anyway?

If you find yourself being rejected over and over again, maybe there *is* a reason. Lynnette is very attractive, but guarded and snippy. She goes on date after date, but no one calls her for a second date.

I say to her, "Maybe you should try to be a little softer."

She snaps back at me, "No, it's that I'm just too intimidating to me."

Well, duh, Lynnette, I think to myself. *Why not try being less intimidating?*

Listen to your friends, family, coworkers and lovers. Read between the lines. They will let you know in subtle ways what it is that you need to change about yourself in order to be happy. Pay attention to the intonation in their voices and their facial expressions.

Develop Personal Magnetism

According to Andrew J. DuBrin, Ph.D., a psychologist and professor of business management at Rochester Institute of Technology, New York and the author of 27 books, including *Personal Magnetism: Discover Your Own Charisma and Learn to Charm, Inspire and Influence Others*, some people have a natural gift for attracting the respect and adoration of others. These people often get what they want in life because they are able to make everyone they meet want to help them succeed. Their secret is "personal magnetism"—that captivating, charismatic quality that attracts people.

Dr. DuBrin spent seven years observing the behavior patterns of charismatic people and what these people did consciously to make other people respond to them positively. He discovered that these behavior patterns could be learned. Here, according to Dr. DuBrin, are the secrets of becoming more magnetic:

- **Be emotionally expressive.** People who control their emotions rarely attract attention. By expressing your emotions in more animated ways, you will seem more interesting and genuine to other people. You are more apt to make a positive impression and people are more likely to remember what you said. How do you become more emotionally expressive? Say how you feel with enthusiasm. Share your positive emotions with others by bringing your words to life with expressions like "I'm thrilled for you!" Even negative statements can be expressed openly and constructively.

- **Communicate extra-verbally.** Make warm eye contact and smile when you talk. Stand straight to give off confidence and magnetism and send a positive message. Hold your arms open so you will appear receptive. Crossed arms make it appear that you are closed and guarded. Use enthusiastic hand gestures.

- **Flatter others.** Put yourself aside and focus on the other person. People crave recognition and appreciation and usually respond favorably to a compliment. Be realistic when using flattery. Be genuine about your compliments. If there is no sincerity behind your comments, the shallowness will be recognized by those to whom you are speaking. Individualize compliments. Just saying "You look great" to everyone seems insincere. Make comments that include details about someone's work or personal life to show that you really care.

- **Be a good listener.** Nothing is more flattering that the active attention of others. Shut off your engines when someone is talking to you. This forces you to focus on what is being said rather than on what you are waiting to say.

- **Quote the other person.** This shows that you have paid attention and that you feel what he does and says are worth taking seriously. "As you put it so well yesterday" is a great form of flattery.

- **Have a sense of humor.** Everyone likes to be around people who make them feel good. We are drawn to those people who relieve our tension, make us feel comfortable, and let us relax and smile. Humor exudes magnetism. You can develop a better sense of humor if you loosen up. Here's how: Look for incongruous elements in everyday situations. Making spontaneous jokes and quips are much more magnetic than reciting rehearsed jokes. Do not be sarcastic. Humor at others' expense does not win friends and influence people. People may laugh at the time, but they will almost always be left with a negative feeling about you. However, self-effacing humor is a long-term winner if you use it sparingly. Laughing at yourself will show other people that you are down to earth and confident in yourself.

- **Laugh.** People who respond to humor and appreciate the wit of others attract more positive attention. Laughter tells others that your personal agenda is not mean-spirited, but rather filled with fun and life.

- **Develop your human side.** Charismatic people are often distinguished by their concern for others. When you show that you care, people will naturally be drawn to you. Here's how: Give others credit for their ideas. By expressing your appreciation you will enhance your own position. Take an interest in the health of others. All magnetic people have this sincere, caring quality. Make sure you always ask how you can be helpful. Be considerate. Before you speak, think about how your comments will make the other person feel. By being considerate you are showing respect, which enhances your magnetism.

Chapter 16

Change Your Attitude

Most of us create our own private misery. We are in a state of chronic anger and need to find a way to change our experience of life to a happier, more positive adventure.

When I go to the market I try to get in the line with Donna, the grocery checker who is always smiling and enjoying what she is doing. She loves chatting with her customers and has gotten to know most of her regulars.

But just one checkout counter away is Becky, a checker who is doing the exact same job as Donna, but her face and body language say that she hates what she is doing. She gets no pleasure from her customers. All she can think of is how much longer until her shift ends.

I feel sorry for Becky. Everyone should enjoy his or her life's work. If you begrudge anything about your work, change it. Don't spend your limited time on this planet doing something that you don't enjoy. And if there is something about your life that you can't change, change your *attitude* about it.

> ❧ *Create a positive attitude about everything in your life and your life will become more positive.* ❧

Choose to Be Loving

In order to understand what love is, we have to understand what love is not. Love is not the act of someone else fulfilling your needs and making you happy. If you believe that finding someone to love you and fulfill your sexual, emotional, physical and financial needs will make you happy, you are dead wrong. You are confusing love with self-gratification.

Charlene has been having an affair with a rich, older, married man for 15 years. She refuses to date anyone else and is wasting her life on a man who admits that he will never leave his wife for her.

"Why are you wasting your life?" I ask her.

"I love him," she replies.

"Does he love you back?" I ask.

"Just look what he gave me," she boasts as she shows me her new diamond stud earrings. How sad, I think, that she believes that this man truly loves her because he gave her expensive earrings. This man has betrayed his wife even though he readily admits that he still loves her. It is clear that his concept of love does not include fidelity. Charlene's self-esteem is so low that she settles for a man who has never and will never spend a weekend or a holiday with her.

Sally is almost 40 years old and her biological clock is ticking, but she has never been married. Although she's very attractive, she has never even had a boyfriend and has no girlfriends left. Every time she begins to develop a relationship with either a girlfriend or a potential male mate, she creates some fight in order to sabotage the relationship. Clearly, she's creating her own self-fulfilling prophecy of being unlovable. Her excuse is that she's a victim of her rich, controlling father.

She runs to adoption agencies and sperm banks, desperate to have a baby. Clearly she thinks that a baby will give her the unconditional love she has never been able to get from her parents, friends or dates.

If you think that having a baby in order to have someone to love you will make you happy, you are dead wrong again. It's like having a chocolate soufflé to cure your cravings for sweets. A few hours later, you crave sweets again. It's like buying a sexy new outfit in order to attract a mate. Once the excitement of the purchase wears off, you still feel the void.

Love is the emotion that allows you to care about another living being more than you care about yourself. To love another person is to take joy in his happiness and to have deep compassion for his pain. It is to overlook what isn't perfect about him and focus on what is good about him. To love another person is to always try to make him feel good about himself.

Do we fall in love? No. Love is an emotion that can only grow from knowing someone very well, which, of course, takes time. Couples who claim it was "love at first sight" usually are referring to the fact that they were attracted to each other and enjoyed each other's company right away. It was infatuation. Love evolves once we get to know what's inside the package and love grows when we learn to trust that person not to hurt us.

Being loved by another is the greatest gift that can be bestowed upon us. What makes some people more lovable than others? A lovable person is sincerely warm, caring, compassionate, trusting, trustworthy, friendly, reliable and giving. An unlovable person only *pretends to be* a lovable person in order to receive the self-gratification he or she is seeking. You cannot hide your motives indefinitely any more than an actor can remain on stage without a break.

If you *choose* to be happy, you must love and be lovable. In order to love others, you must love yourself. And, in order to love yourself, you must really like and trust yourself.

If you *choose* to be happy, let go of your preconceived ideas about what love is and how a person should show his love for you. When the person who is supposed to love you does not show you love in the way you think love should be shown, you must remind yourself to allow that person to love you in the way that *he* knows how to love.

Recently, two extremely materialistic women I know—one single, one divorced—asked me what my husband got for me for Valentines Day. When I said, "He brought me some flowers, a card, and we went out for a nice, romantic dinner," their faces clouded over with pity.

One asked, "No jewelry?"

I replied, "Business isn't good, and besides, he doesn't need to buy me jewelry in order to prove that he loves me."

These two women looked at me in disbelief. In their minds, if a man loves you he gives you expensive gifts. In my mind, true love is give and take, understanding, trust, sharing and compassion. It is to put another's needs before my own materialistic needs. My husband and I will grow old together, walking down the street hand in hand when we are 90 years old. These women will still be searching for love. But how can they find love when they cannot understand what love really is?

A person may actually be incapable of love if he doesn't love himself. He is probably aware at some level that he is unlovable because he knows that deep down inside his soul he is not kind, caring and compassionate.

Sometimes these people who can't love don't have a conscience.

They can hurt you emotionally and physically and not even feel the slightest tinge of guilt or remorse. They always have some illogical rationale for treating you disrespectfully. Sometimes these are the people who profess their love for you the loudest. But one act of kindness is worth saying "I love you" a thousand times. These people don't love you; they are manipulating you into loving them so that they will feel better about themselves. After all, the more people they can manipulate into loving them the more lovable they must be, right? *Wrong.*

If a person professes his love for you and yet continues to hurt you, he really doesn't love you. People don't hurt people they love under any circumstances.

> ❧ *To allow someone to treat you disrespectfully is to disrespect yourself. You cannot be happy if you disrespect yourself.* ❧

If you have a mate who is continually hurting you emotionally and/or physically, he doesn't love you any more than he loves himself. He is just using your love for his own self-gratification.

Ana is always unhappy because her husband, Peter, is mean and insensitive to her. They just came back from a trip to Mexico and the plane ride was turbulent. Ana, frightened, asked Peter to hold her hand. He refused to hold her hand and ridiculed her by asking, "Didn't anyone ever teach you how to act on an airplane?"

Peter is always trying to make Ana feel as if there is something wrong with her. If he loved her, wouldn't he feel kindness, caring and compassion for her fears rather than try to make her feel worse? Yet, Ana has been putting up with this degradation for 15 years because she believes Peter loves her. He has made her feel so insecure that she believes that if she leaves him she will never find anyone else who will love her. Peter might need Ana, but he certainly doesn't love her. People just don't degrade people they love.

Can you stop loving someone you once loved? *Yes.* If you love someone but that person only hurts you over and over again, you will eventually learn that he does not and probably cannot love you in return no matter how many times he says, "I love you." Actions always speak louder than words. The words "I love you" are meaningless when the person's actions show no caring, kindness or compassion.

When you let go of the people in your life who really don't love you and who are hurting you, you open yourself up for love from other sources and you will eventually find the quality of love and friendship you deserve. If you allow a person who professes that he loves you to continue to hurt you, you are sabotaging your own happiness by allowing him to harm you.

Love cannot flourish without trust. If you think that you love a person who is not trustworthy, you are wrong. You only think you love him or her because he or she satisfies some of your needs.

If you love your teenage or adult child but he or she is continually hurting you, your love diminishes until the act of loving your child becomes just a moral obligation that you feel guilty not fulfilling. If a person hurts you enough, you will finally stop loving him or her.

Kelly believes that her parents should love her unconditionally, but Kelly is a pathological liar. She has stolen many things from her own parents. She has been in jail twice. She is a narcissist who never stops talking about herself. She has been verbally and physically abusive to her parents in the past. Isn't it funny how someone like Kelly, who believes in unconditional love, is constantly testing others' love for her to its limit?

Does Kelly think that she can treat her parents disrespectfully—cheat, lie, steal, scream, abuse—and yet, her parents are obliged to still love her? Should a child love a parent who abuses him or her verbally, emotionally or physically? There is no law that you have to love a parent or a child unconditionally. Even a dog turns on its owner when it can finally take no more abuse.

How do you accept that a person you love does not act kindly to you or love you back? Perhaps she doesn't have the capacity to love you back because she doesn't love herself. Maybe she is incapable of feeling compassion. Possibly there is an evil that lurks inside her that she can't control. Conceivably, she just plain doesn't love you—or anyone.

There are those that would argue that there is good inside everyone, even the most vicious of killers. And that might be true. One might be able to find an inkling of good inside even the most evil person. In reverse, there is usually an inkling of evil inside even the most kind and caring person. But what really matters is how a person, *any* person, is affecting *your* happiness.

*❧ If you **choose** to be happy you must choose to believe that **no one** has a right to make you unhappy. ❧*

Trust and Betrayal

In order to truly love a person you must trust him 100%. If he truly loves you in return, he will not betray your trust. The pain of hurting you, the person he loves, is much stronger than any possible temptation.

If someone in your life has professed his love for you and yet has betrayed your trust, you have no choice other than to accept the reality that he really doesn't love you. He might love being with you. He might love being loved by you. He might love what you do for him or give to him, but a person who has betrayed you does not love you. If he loved you, he would not hurt you.

Once you have been betrayed, you can never trust that person again. You will always have the knowledge that if he was capable of betraying you once, he is capable of betraying you again.

The quickest way to regain happiness after you have been betrayed is to learn to trust again. Because you were deceived and hurt by someone does not mean that the next person will betray and hurt you. Judge each person you meet on his or her own merits. Even in our legal system, a person is innocent until proven guilty.

How do you protect yourself from being hurt again? Nothing will guarantee that you will not be betrayed again short of eliminating all human contact for the rest of your life.

Is Love Always Forever?

Nancy married Larry thinking he was her knight in shining armor. She really believed that he would rescue her from her financial and emotional distress. She believed that another human being could make her life the way she had always dreamed it should be.

It is now 20 years later and her knight in shining armor has turned into a pawn in tarnished aluminum. He has gone from job to job getting fired from each and every one of them and they have gone through their life savings trying to stay one step ahead of the collection agencies. Nancy had to start her own business and works 15 hours a day just to make ends meet and pay off old debts. Now older, faced with the disappointment of not achieving her dream life, and tired of the financial problems, she realizes that she is no longer in love with this man. What should she do?

It used to be that when a person made a commitment to spend the rest of her life with another person, it was an irreversible decision. Divorce was unthinkable. Nowadays, one out of every two first marriages ends in divorce and two out of three second marriages end in divorce. Obviously, not everyone is taking his or her wedding vows seriously.

Can you fall out of love when your loved one does not live up to your expectations? *Yes,* but, maybe it is your unfulfilled lofty expectations that are making you unhappy rather than your mate. If it is your unrealistic expectations that are making you discontented, you are bound to repeat this pattern again even if you leave your mate and find another one.

Nancy's problem has its roots in the original idea that Larry was going to fulfill all of her fantasies and make her happy. What she didn't understand at the time that she married him was that no one but *you* can make *you* happy. Maybe she wasn't really in love with him, but rather the lavish lifestyle that he convinced her he was going to provide.

So does Nancy have to grin and bear it and live with someone she has no respect for because he can't make a living? Should she leave, knowing there aren't too many men looking for middle-aged women with whom to share their money? And if that man came along, he would have his own set of problems that might be worse than the problems she has now.

Sometimes our lives don't turn out the way we would have wanted them to turn out. This is disappointing. Nancy is disappointed. At what age do you evaluate how your life turned out?

❧ As long as you wake up breathing your life
hasn't turned out any way yet. As long as you have a goal,
you are still in the game. ❧

Negate Hate

Racial hatred is fear in disguise. Why does the Klu Klux Klan hate African Americans and Jews? Because they fear them. Why do different species of animals hate each other? Because prey fears its predators.

In order to stop hating we must all learn the art of empathy. We should always strive to put ourselves in the other person's shoes and experience life through his or her eyes.

> ❧ *Happiness and hate can't coexist. To hate is to*
> *sabotage your own happiness. Hate begets hate.* ❧

The television program *Dateline* once did an experiment in which they sent out an African American woman and a Caucasian woman— both the same age, both dressed equally well—into a shoe store to buy some shoes. The white woman got immediate attention while the African American woman was ignored.

In another experiment, an African American man and a Caucasian man were sent on an interview for the same job. Each was equally qualified and equally as attractive and well-dressed. The Caucasian got the job. *Dateline* did several other experiments, all of which made me realize what it might be like to not be treated equally in our society.

I was really able to empathize with what it must feel like to be discriminated against all the time. I was more able to understand how an African American or any other discriminated-against minority might feel every single day of his or her life.

In the last two decades, Los Angeles has become a very multi-cultural society. People from other countries have been flowing into our city, bringing with them many diverse cultures. But as the number of immigrants grows, the wonderful city I have lived in since I was 13 years old has become filled with graffiti and crime. I can't even drive down the freeway without worrying about being shot. I must admit, I used to be angry. My anger manifested itself as hate. Hate for anyone who ruined my city and the quality of my life. I knew my anger was affecting my happiness, so I decided to try to see the world through others' eyes.

I was brought up in a two-parent family. My father was a doctor and my mother a college-educated housewife. We lived in a home in an upper middleclass neighborhood of Los Angeles. What would it have been like if my father had been a drug addict or an alcoholic? What if he had beaten up my mother or molested me? What would it have been like if he ran off and my mother had to raise us alone? What if she had to go on welfare? What if she was a drug addict, alcoholic, or prostitute? What if there was never enough to eat? What if every time I walked out my front door I heard gunshots or I watched the police putting the next door neighbor in handcuffs? What if when I went to school I never learned anything because the teachers were too busy disciplining other students? What if every time I looked at a magazine or a billboard or watched television or a movie I saw people with things that I thought that I could never have? What if every time I passed a woman, she clutched her purse in fear that I would steal it from her?

The vast majority of the people living in the ghettos are hardworking people who are just trying to raise their families the best that they can and have a decent life amid the chaos of the crime-ridden streets.

I think of my Vietnamese manicurist, who works seven days a week, 12 hours a day, to raise her four children alone, smiling with pride as she shows me a picture of her son in his U.S. Marine uniform.

I think of the girls working for our cleaning service who clean five or six houses a day and then go home and take care of their own families.

I think of the Korean family who own the local grocery store and work seven days a week, 16 hours a day, so that they can send their children to college.

The more we understand another culture the more empathy we have for its differences. Empathy is the first step to eradicating hate. If we have empathy for the conditions in which other people have grown up and learn to understand their thought processes, we can understand their anger. And if we can understand their anger, whether or not it is justified, we can let go of our own anger.

Never use the word "hate." Hate eats away at you like a cancer. You are only hurting yourself by hating. In order to stop hating, learn to forgive those you think have wronged you. This doesn't mean that you have to accept the behavior you are forgiving; it just means that you have to forgive the behavior so you can go on to enjoy your life.

*❧ Delete the word "hate" from your vocabulary.
"Hate" is the worst four-letter word. It is **toxic**. ❧*

Have Compassion and Empathy

If you *choose* to be happy, replace your hate and anger with empathy and compassion. Compassion comes to you when you stop being self-centered and self-absorbed—when everything that happens does not have to do with *you*. Compassion is the ability to see another human being's pain and want to help him. It is a prerequisite to being happy.

Empathy is the ability to put oneself in another person's place and to be able to feel his pain. Learn to have kindness towards and understand others who behave or think differently than you.

John Stossel did a report on *20/20* several years ago on African Americans and what they thought Caucasians were doing to them. I was appalled to find out that many African Americans, some very well educated, thought that the "K" on Snapple stands for Klu Klux Klan (it stands for "kosher.") That Church's fried chicken was formulated to sterilize black men; that AZT was formulated to heal white men and kill black men; and that crack cocaine was being supplied to the black community by our government in order to commit genocide.

I finally *really* understood how differently people think and interpret facts. I tried to think what it would be like if I had been born black and had heard these tales all my life. I realized that I might believe them too.

With the growth of white supremacist groups in the U.S., neo-Nazism in Germany, and radical Islamists in the U.S. and abroad, hate is growing stronger. How can you hate a group of people you don't even know? How can you hate a person who has been fed different information all his life? How can you hate a person just because he thinks or acts or talks or looks differently than you? People only hate people they fear. Fear comes from ignorance and unfounded beliefs.

I am not saying that we should empathize with terrorists and neo-Nazis, but I am saying that we should try to understand why they think as they do.

Reject Revenge

How do you stop hating those who have personally hurt you? A lover who has scorned you or cheated on you? A parent who has abandoned you? An ungrateful child who has disappointed and mistreated you, who takes from you and never gives you anything but unhappiness in return? A relative who has molested you? A con artist who has scammed you out of your life savings? A friend who has betrayed your trust? A boss who has fired you for no reason? A drunk driver who has hit you and crippled you or killed a loved one? Criminals who bilk our government out of millions of our tax dollars?

Thoughts of revenge do not punish your offender and make him unhappy, but rather they punish *you* and make *you* unhappy.

❧ *If you **choose** to be happy, **let go** of your vengeful thoughts.* ❧

It doesn't matter whether you are right or wrong. It doesn't matter whether the person who hurt you is good or bad. It doesn't matter whether the system is just or unjust. You have been granted the wisdom to change those things you can change and accept those things you cannot change.

There is probably no logical or personal reason why anyone would want to hurt you. Generally, it's not the desire to hurt you personally that motivates a person, but rather the inability of a person to control his or her own impulses.

Planning revenge and retaliation only creates negative emotion and energy. If you can believe that life is fair, that in the end everyone must pay the price for his or her behavior, then you can hand over the punishment responsibility to your Higher Spirit and free up your energy to live your life happily.

Anger is usually hurt in disguise. Ex-spouses are angry with their ex-spouses because they hurt them emotionally, physically and/or financially. When you say something to a person and he gets angry with you, it is usually because you said something that hurt him. You can't be happy until you let go of your own anger (which is really hurt) and refuse to see yourself as a victim anymore. Move on with your life and stop blaming someone else for your unhappiness.

One of the women prisoners in the movie *Paradise Road* said, "I've never met a person I can hate."

"Why?" asked another female prisoner.

"Because the meaner and nastier someone is the sorrier I feel for him."

Decide not to hate anyone or anything because it is impossible to hate and be happy at the same time.

Good vs. Evil

In my favorite book, Stephen King's *The Stand*, a virus wiped out most of mankind and the only survivors fought the ultimate war between good and evil. There has always been evil and there will always be evil. It is just the way of the Universe. If there is up, there must be down. If there is black, there must be white. If there is good, there must be evil.

Many religions believe that those who believe in Jesus Christ as the messiah are good and that Satan possesses the souls of those who don't believe in Jesus. Religions such as Islam believe in the teachings of the Koran. Radical Islamists interpret this as meaning that all of those who believe in Allah are good and will go to heaven and all those who do not believe in Allah are bad and will go to hell.

Most ideologies—good and bad—have to do with cultural values. Many other cultures have much stronger family bonds than Americans do, and yet in their culture it is okay to tell a lie in business. In other cultures, a person's life has much less value than in the United States. In some parts of the Middle East, the "family honor" is so important that if an unmarried girl has sex prior to marriage, even if she is raped, the oldest son is ordered by the father to kill her because she has disgraced the family.

Does it make it evil when a person is just doing what he has been taught and what his ancestors have been doing for years? Can these people be truly happy if they lie and cheat in business? If they kill another human being for the sake of their religious beliefs?

I personally believe that no one can be truly happy unless he can go to sleep at night knowing that he has lived his day with integrity and has not hurt another human being or animal.

But our job is not to judge or procure the happiness of everyone. It's too big of a job and we just don't have that much power. Just working on our own happiness and helping the people we love to be happy is hard enough.

All conflict in the world is based on the struggle between good and evil. A man who shoots and kills a doctor who performs abortions believes that he is destroying evil. He cannot see that his own act of killing is evil. Terrorists believe Americans are evil just as much as we believe that they are evil. It is evident that it is much easier to perceive evil in others than it is to perceive evil in ourselves.

Most people believe that they themselves are basically good. The nurse you hired to take care of your mother with Alzheimer's disease steals her money and jewelry. In the nurse's mind, she is entitled to steal because she believes that she is underpaid. The babysitter you hired to take care of your baby abuses your infant. In the babysitter's mind, the baby deserves to be abused because he or she is bothering the babysitter.

How can we be happy when we have to share our world with people who think like this? Because we have no choice if we want to be happy. There have always been and there will always be people who have distorted logic. If we *choose* to be happy we must accept the distorted logic because we just can't change how others think.

Stop Being a Victim

Several years ago my husband and I found out that one of his long lost cousins had inserted herself into his 105 year old father's life and had tricked him into changing his will and trust in favor of her. She was even making up lies to turn my husband's father against his own son. We felt overwhelming anger toward this woman. It was physically and emotionally draining. My back and neck muscles were in spasm all the time and I had a constant headache. How could we let go of the anger?

We tried to have compassion for her desperation and greed. We felt better about ourselves, but it didn't solve the problem. We tried believing that our Higher Spirit would make sure that justice would prevail, but were reminded of O. J. Simpson smiling on the golf course right after he was acquitted. We tried isolating this fight from the rest of our lives, but we couldn't stop thinking about what this woman was trying to get away with. The anger got worse.

I realized that the anger we were feeling towards this woman was making us sick. We had to let go and just relax. We decided to think of it as a game of chess. I remembered that the best defense is a good offense. Instead of letting her get away with this underhanded act and feeling like helpless victims, we hired an attorney and decided to put her in checkmate. By feeling in *control* of the problem instead of like victims, we were able to *let go* of our anger.

Prosperity Is Only a State of Mind

If you think you are poor, you are poor. If you think you are rich, you are rich. If you think small, your rewards in life will be meager. If you think big, you will create abundance. You create your own opportunity. You create your own limitations. The Universe has a way of giving you what you ask for—although, sometimes not in the exact way you were expecting it.

Money is merely something that you use to exchange for goods or services so that you can enjoy your life. It can be green paper printed by the government or it can be the plastic beads they use at Club Med. If you cling to your money because you are afraid that you won't be able to make any more, you create your own reality of lack of money. If you are afraid to use your money for your own pleasure, you are denying yourself the rewards of life.

Worrying about money is normal. *Obsessing* over money is not normal or healthy. There is nothing wrong with doing everything you can to make money as long as it is honest, moral and ethical. However, pursuing money as your main focus in life will make you unhappy.

Money buys financial security, power, control and freedom. It buys comfortable lifestyles, travel, beautiful possessions, fast cars, jewelry and boats. It buys freedom from doing things that are against your ethics.

> ❧ *Money **cannot** buy happiness,*
> *but the lack of money **can** make you unhappy.* ❧

Many offspring of the richest people in the world are the unhappiest people in the world because they were given everything in life when they were very young. They have nothing to strive for and nothing to look forward to because they have already "been there, seen it, done it."

As a very wealthy friend of my husband and I says, "Money doesn't make you happy unless you don't have any."

Success Is the Quality of Your Journey

You are a unique individual with strengths and weaknesses. In our society, success is often measured by how much money someone makes. Judging yourself by how much money you make will make you unhappy whether you do or you don't reach your financial goals.

❧ *If you enjoy your life, you are successful.* ❧

Stop Blaming Yourself

Okay, so you are selfish. Everyone is selfish. Everything everyone does is for some kind of self-gratification, no matter how indirect. When you give a gift to someone, it makes you feel good to give to that person. Therefore, gift giving is selfish.

If you have done or said something that you feel guilty about, do what you can to apologize and make amends to the person or persons that you have hurt. Vow to yourself that you will never ever again knowingly do or say anything that will make you feel guilty.

❧ *Guilt cannot coexist with happiness.* ❧

Stop Putting Off Happiness

When you were a child you could not wait until you grew up so you parents would not tell you what you could and couldn't do. You thought you would finally be happy when you were an adult.

When you graduated from school and were out on your own you couldn't wait until you found that perfect someone. You thought you would finally be happy when you got married.

After you were married for a while you couldn't wait until you had a baby. You thought that you would finally be happy when you had your own family.

When your children were growing up, you couldn't wait until they were old enough to go away to school. You thought you would be happy if you could just have some time for yourself.

When your children got married and left home, you couldn't wait until you could retire. You thought that if you were retired you wouldn't have any responsibilities and that you would finally be happy.

So now you and your gray-haired spouse are driving somewhere through some cornfields in your brand new motor home looking for a place to park for the night and you finally realize you have no problems. Now, you are bored to tears and wish for the "good old days."

❧ Happiness is not something tangible that you can achieve, like a trophy. It is a way of thinking. It is an ongoing process. ❧

Coping With a Traumatic Event

There comes a time in almost everyone's life when he or she is faced with a real trauma. You ask yourself, "Why me?" "What did I do to deserve this?" "Will my life ever be normal again?" "How long can I take this?" "Is this a bad dream?" It can be the death of a loved one, a divorce, a disease, an accident or a financial disaster. Very few people reach old age without experiencing one or more of these traumas. How do you regain your happiness?

- Express your anger. Ask "Why did this happen to me?" The answer is because you are a member of the human race. No one is exempt from tragedy. Don't misplace your anger and hurt on the very people who love you and are there to help you. You will only be hurting yourself more.

- Accept what happened. This event will probably change your life. Accept that change is inevitable. Try to see it as a challenge and a growing experience. Strive to see the new opportunities that might open themselves up to you because of this trauma.

- Allow yourself to grieve. Pamper yourself. Allow others to be kind to you. Talk about it. Keep a journal. Give yourself an allotment of time in order to go through this process. When that ration of time is over, it is time to move on with your life.

- Do what it is you need to do. Whether it's funeral arrangements and/or reorganizing and restructuring your whole life, get started. If your mind is occupied with moving forward it will have a bad time dwelling on the past.

- Let it go. Your life must go on. Trying to find justice in an unjust world is an exercise in futility. Why not spend your time and energy in making your life happy?

- Learn the lessons that this event is trying to teach you. Try to turn it into a positive. Use your ordeal to do something that will better the quality of life for all of mankind. Christopher Reeve worked to get more government funding for spinal injury victims. Denise Brown works to get support to stop spousal abuse. In this way, you can give the traumatic event a reason to have happened.

Abusive Relationships

Lorna is in an abusive relationship. The man she lives with flies into uncontrollable rages. The intellectual part of her realizes that he will never change. The emotional part of her lets him do this to her and makes excuses to herself and others for his behavior. She does not have the strength and courage to leave him. When asked "Why do you allow him to treat you this way?" she replies "Well, he's under so much stress at work." You should never have to make excuses for your mate's behavior.

Women who sell their souls for the love of a mate have very low self-esteem, as do men who sell their souls for the love of a woman. No human being has a right to treat you poorly.

How do you draw the line between behavior that you are willing to put up with and behavior you are not willing to put up with? Women get PMS and are unreasonable once in a while. Men have testosterone rises that make them go into rages every once in a while. Do we leave someone just because they have hormonal mood swings? Only you know what you are willing to put up with. Only you know the positives (and the negatives) of your relationship.

If you are afraid of this person, then it is time to leave. No one should have to live his or her life in fear. If this person is making you unhappy, it is time to leave. No one has the right to make your life unhappy. If this person is trying to control you, it is time to leave. Control can be subtle. Turning you against your friends or family is a strong clue that this person is trying to control you.

Love Yourself

If you *choose* to be happy you must love yourself. In order to love yourself you must first like yourself. How do you learn to like yourself? Simple—just be the kind of likeable person you would like to spend time with. There are many universally likeable traits.

- Be your authentic self.

- Be honest, warm, sincere, friendly, even-tempered, courteous, well mannered, fun, lighthearted, bright, interesting, concerned, helpful, compassionate and loving.

- Always do your best to make others feel good about themselves.

- Be a good listener.

- Don't be self-absorbed with your own problems all the time.

- Be clean, neat and attractive.

- Develop your social graces.

- Be positive.

- Don't complain.

- Be enthusiastic and enjoy all of life's experiences.

- Be moral. You know the difference between right and wrong behavior. You know your moral duty and obligations. Always choose the right behavior even if the consequences don't bring you immediate gratification. Just knowing that you have chosen the right behavior is reward enough in itself. If you choose wrong behavior by accident, first, accept and admit to yourself and whomever you need to apologize to that you have made a mistake. Second, forgive yourself for being human and making that mistake. Third, learn from that mistake and make a vow never to make that same mistake again. Always *choose* the right behavior no matter what you have to give up and what the consequences are.

- Be ethical. Always do what you believe is fair. You will not be able to love yourself if you have lied, cheated, been dishonest or tricked anyone into buying something or doing something that was not in his or her best interests. In order to love yourself you must have a clear conscience and that doesn't mean doing whatever you want, right or wrong, and then counting on being forgiven.

- Act with integrity. Develop your own moral beliefs and convictions. In order to act with integrity you must adhere to that moral code no matter what.

- Act with conscience. If you are a good person you know when you do not abide by your moral code. You know when you are dishonest. You know when you have hurt someone. The element that separates a good person like you from a bad person is that a bad person feels no guilt. He can commit an immoral act or hurt someone and not feel guilt or remorse. Because he does not experience these feelings, he does not learn from his experiences. Good people feel guilt and shame when they have acted wrongly. These feelings are painful and should be because pain is what makes you learn from your mistakes and grow to be a better person. Just the process of growing to be a better person can make you happy.

- Find a mentor. Emulate people you admire who are doing good things for society.

It doesn't matter if your parents told you that you were not good enough. It doesn't matter if your friends and family tell you that you are not worth loving. If you act in such a way that is moral and ethical and if you have integrity, you can go to sleep liking and loving yourself. You know that you are a good person and that's all that is important. Many times other people are not even aware of the good things that we do. Think of all the philanthropists who give millions of dollars to charity and don't want anyone to know. Why? Because the act of giving and helping mankind is reward enough. If you have a good heart and follow your heart, you will be rewarded with happiness by just knowing you are good.

Chapter 17

Create Your Own Good Luck

Sometimes life appears to be unfair. Bad things happen to good people. Good things happen to bad people. If you *choose* to be happy, you must believe that bad things happen as a catalyst to bring about good changes. That everything happens for an ultimate reason

Nicole Simpson and Ron Goldman had to die in order for society to realize that it needed to do something about spousal abuse. O. J. had to be found not guilty in order for us to see how unfair our judicial system can be. Christopher Reeve had to have his accident in order to speed up finding a cure for spinal cord injuries. Princess Diana had to die so that people would really pay attention to the causes she supported.

It's no accident that the human body is designed with two of almost everything: two arms, two legs, two eyes, two nostrils, two ears, two kidneys, two ovaries and so on. And it's no accident that nature is a perfect balance between plants and animals and that the seasons come at the same time every year; that the days and nights arrive like clockwork—no pun intended; that a woman's body automatically menstruates every 28 days. If every cell in nature has an ultimate reason to exist, isn't it logically possible that every event in your life has a reason?

If you *choose* to be happy, it is necessary to believe that when something bad happens to you, no matter how awful that event is, it will create a positive result in the end. If you can accept this principle, you will be able to be happy in spite of the bad things that are bound to happen to you during your lifetime.

Coincidences Are No Coincidence

Everything that happens to you is supposed to happen for a reason. Perhaps you read *The Celestine Prophecy* by James Redfield? The premise of the book is that every coincidence in life has a meaning and that there are no chance encounters. If you run into someone, it's because you are supposed to learn something from your encounter with this person.

I once went through a two-or three-year period when I ran into just about everyone I had ever known during my first marriage. What I discovered from each and every one of these chance encounters was *the truth*. I had previously *perceived* that these friendships didn't endure after my divorce because they were taking sides and chose to be friends with my ex-husband over me. What I learned from my chance encounters was that my *perception* was totally wrong—these people were all misreading my unhappiness and thinking that it was I who didn't want to be friends with them.

By accepting the principle that every event in our lives has a meaning, I was able to see that these chance encounters were learning experiences that were meant to heal my wounds and make me see how my own negative thoughts had been affecting my happiness.

I had also thought that these people all had gone on to lead fairytale lives and that I was the only one who had had major problems. What I discovered was that every one of them had his or her own set of problems and that none of their lives has been a fairytale, as I had imagined.

In some circumstances, I tried to renew friendships that had ended for reasons I didn't remember. Once into the renewed friendships, I realized the reasons why these friendships hadn't endured; we just had the wrong chemistry.

I like to think of people's personalities, or cores, as being classified as a number one to a number ten, no number being any better or worse than any other number. Some people are ones, while others are fours, or sevens or tens. Ones relate the best to ones just as tens relate the best to tens. A one will relate better to a two than it will relate to a ten. A ten will relate better to a nine than it will to a one. This explains why you will connect to some people immediately and have nothing in common with other people no matter how hard you try.

I also had a period when I ran into a lot of people that I had known in high school. I had always *felt* unpopular in my adolescence, although in hindsight, I wasn't unpopular at all. It was just my *perception*. What I learned from each of these chance encounters was that there was nothing wrong with me back then. Rather, my own feelings of inadequacy were self-inflicted and had bothered me for a good part of my life. In each instance, every chance encounter cleared up a false belief that had been in my mind all of these years. In the end, I feel so much better about my own life and myself. Of course, now I know the reasons why I was running into all of those people.

❧ *There are no coincidences.* ❧

The Purpose of Life

I believe there are two purposes for our lives. First, you live in order to contribute to the advancement and betterment of mankind in some small way. Second, you are alive to enjoy that process and to be happy.

Life is always changing. Therefore, life itself is a perpetual learning process. We will never reach a point of ultimate bliss because without problems to solve there is no reason to live. The quest for the solution to problems is the energy, the driving force that makes us want to live and to create.

Do you think Stephen Spielberg really needs to make more money? I highly doubt it. He keeps on making more movies because the creativity, the challenge of entertaining people, the quest to make better and better movies is what drives him. He needs the challenges to make him feel alive—and so do you!

Trust Your Intuition

It is the strongest sense you have. Intuition is that little voice inside of you that always knows what is right. It is your inner-self guiding you to make the correct choice or decision. Your first impression about someone or something is usually the most accurate impression.

It has been shown that when students guess an answer on an exam, their first guess has the best probability of being correct. It has been also been proven that most people form an opinion about another person in the first few seconds that they meet. That gut feeling you get about someone or something is a natural instinct. It's similar to a dog knowing that you are a dog lover or a horse knowing that you aren't afraid of it.

I have discovered a little voice inside of me. If I ask questions, this voice gives me answers. I don't know whether this voice is my own brain, my subconscious, my Higher Power, my imagination, or if I need to be institutionalized, but I do know that this little voice contains much wisdom, which I have called my *intuition*. I always listen to this little voice. It is *always* right.

We all have a sixth sense, but some people develop it better than others do. It is just that "little feeling" that something is not right. Develop your sixth sense. Pay attention to that "little feeling"—it is telling you something very important. The more in touch you are with that little feeling, the fewer mistakes you will make about the people you allow into your life as well as the investments and career choices you make.

Have you ever known that someone was going to call and then the phone rings and it's that person? Have you ever distrusted a person you just met even though he seemed pleasant and sincere? You can't put your finger on why you know something, but you know it. This is your sixth sense. It's your inner voice combined with your gut feelings, subtle vibes, past experiences and keen observation.

If it doesn't feel right, it isn't right. That little voice inside your head that does not stop talking all day is your Higher Spirit. It is your subconscious mind guiding your conscious mind.

When you are angry and about to lash out at the object of your anger, take the time to have a dialogue with your inner voice about what the consequences of your angry words will be. Talk with your inner voice about what motivates the person who is the object of your anger. Understand her point of view. Have compassion for what makes her react the way she does. Learn to communicate with your inner voice. It will guide you to respond in ways that will make your life happier and more successful. Listen to this inner voice. It is your guardian angel.

Pay Attention to Omens

Sometimes the Universe gives you clues as to what is going to happen. If you ignore those clues, you will undoubtedly get into trouble.

For instance, many years ago I was leaving the next morning on a ski trip to Utah. The bulb in our nightlight had burned out and in the middle of the night I walked right into a wall, toes first, on the way to the bathroom. My big toe turned black and swelled up like a giant plum. My husband took me to the emergency room. Luckily my toe wasn't broken, but this was "Omen Number One."

The next morning we left on our ski trip, not paying attention to this omen. The following day we went skiing at the Alta resort in Utah. On my way back from the bathroom I was coming down the stairs, holding on to the wooden railing, and I got a big splinter in my hand. We went to the first aid room of the ski resort. They didn't even have a tweezers to get out the splinter. My husband said, "I sure hope we don't end up in here with a *real* emergency." "Omen Number Two."

Again, ignoring the second omen, we went skiing. On the way down the mountain, an out-of-control skier came skiing down the hill out of nowhere and plowed into me, knocking me to the ground. My bindings didn't release and my leg twisted as I fell, causing my tibia to twist into two pieces, jutting out of my leg like a wounded soldier in some bloody war movie.

I had a compound spiral fracture of the tibia and had to be taken in a gondola down the hill, where I was taken by ambulance to a local hospital where I had several operations. After 10 months, three operations, a lot of pain, inconvenience and money, I was functioning semi-normally and had a complete hardware store in my leg.

What was the lesson? I should have paid attention to the omens. The Universe was telling me that I shouldn't ski anymore and that something was going to happen to make sure I didn't.

Another eerie example is the recurrent dreams my mother used to have. She used to call every morning and tell me she was upset because she had a dream about being lost. I believe this was an omen about getting Alzheimer's disease, which she developed soon after.

Yet another example was when we bought our home. I was anxious to buy a home instead of lease. I was inheriting some money from my aunt, but the process of probate was taking much longer than I anticipated. The real estate brokers were rushing me to close escrow so they could get their commissions. The omens were there: The water on the wall that the owner and real estate brokers insisted was just from watering a plant. The money for the down payment wasn't available on time. But I didn't pay attention to these omens. I rushed the probate and closed escrow.

First, the bottom fell out of the real estate market in Los Angeles and the condominium was worth much less than we paid for it. Next, we found out that there was water on the wall because there were no flashings in the windows. The builder had made many construction mistakes and later our condominium association filed a lawsuit against the builder. Then, there was a murder in one of the units and the value of that unit dropped, affecting the value of our unit even more. The following week I found out that the city was going to build a Little League baseball field right in front of our house. If only I had known then to pay attention to omens.

Another example of multiple omens is how John Denver had two previous airplane accidents prior to the one that took his life. He had even had his pilot's license revoked. Unfortunately, he didn't pay attention to the omens that were practically beating him over his head.

When someone or something "just doesn't feel right," walk away. When things happen to prevent you from doing something, don't force it to happen. How many times have you heard stories about people who just missed their plane and later found out that the plane they would have been on had crashed?

Don't force anything to happen that doesn't happen easily. Don't force anyone to marry you if he or she doesn't want to. Don't force having a baby if you can't get pregnant. Don't force a business venture that is not falling into place easily.

❧ *If something is meant to be, it will happen easily.* ❧

Be Aware of What Life Is Trying to Tell You:

- Pay attention to the people in your life. The behavior and traits that you don't like in other people are the exact behavior and traits that you don't like about yourself.

- Pay attention to yourself. What is it you are doing or not doing to create the positive and negative energy in your life?

- Pay attention to your body. It is sending you messages. If you suffer from headaches or stomach aches, you are allowing your environment to put too much stress on you. Pain is nature's way of warning you to make changes in your lifestyle before the stress causes a major disease.

- Pay attention to Mother Nature. Earthquakes, hurricanes, tornadoes, brutal winter storms, floods and fires are all Mother Nature's way of warning us to be much gentler and kinder to each other. If mankind doesn't heed Mother Nature's warning, she will keep on showing her fury until we get her message.

If you do not learn from your mistakes you will keep on making the same mistakes over and over again until you finally learn life's lessons.

Life Is Cyclical

The seasons change from summer to fall to winter to spring year after year, century after century. Flowers bloom and die according to the seasons. Animals are born, reproduce, raise their offspring, and die. The financial world and the real estate market are based on cycles of depression, recessions and booms.

If all of life is cyclical then it is logical that your life is cyclical, too. Your moods are cyclical. Your successes and failures are cyclical. That means that perhaps you've gone through cycles in your life when everything you did seemed to work out great and perhaps now you are going through a cycle where nothing you do seems to work out right. Haven't you experienced feast or famine at one time or another in your life? You either had no date on Saturday night or you had too many and you didn't know which one to choose? Or you couldn't find a job for three months and one day you had three job offers?

If you acknowledge that your life is cyclical and that perhaps you are going through a bad cycle, you can *choose* to be happy by accepting that this negative cycle will end at some point and a good cycle will begin.

Luck is cyclical, too. You can go to one blackjack table after another, play every hand according to the book, and lose every hand one day. The next day you can sit at the same table for hours on end and, no matter how many mistakes you make, you keep on winning. If you learn to bet big when the cycle is going your way and to back off when the cycle is against you, you will end up a winner. Learn to back off and ride out your bad cycles patiently and to bet heavily when your good cycles return. Not just at a gambling table, but in the game of life.

Friendships

The quantity and quality of your friendships is usually an accurate measure of your inner success. I'm not talking about the social climbers, the acquaintances that latch on to financially successful and famous people only to disappear when they have fallen from grace. I'm talking about the true friends that you cultivate on your path through life—the friendships that endure the ups and downs that most lives must withstand.

Friends are meant to enhance your life, not to drain you and make you unhappy. The quality of your friendships is much more important than padding your Christmas party list or filling those empty chairs at your funeral.

Balance

As an ex-interior designer, I understand the importance of the balance in a room. Good balance creates a sense of well-being. There is always balance in nature. The Chinese art of Feng Shui practices balance between man and his environment.

You cannot be happy unless you have balance in your life. There should be a balance between alone time and social time, work time and play time, and hedonistic pursuits and religious observance.

We all tend to divide our lives into categories—love, family, friends, money, career, home, car, hobbies, sports and so forth. There are so many different aspects of our lives, the odds of you being completely satisfied with every aspect of your life at any one time is close to impossible. All of us fall short in one or more of these areas. If you *choose* to be happy you must accept the fact that you are only human and that your life cannot be perfect in every area.

Learn to enjoy the life you have been blessed with and to ignore the things or people in your life that are less than perfect.

Go on a "News Diet"

Every morning since the attacks of 9/11 I get up and turn on the news, only to learn about another suicide bombing in the Middle East, another child abducted, or another earthquake that kills five hundred people. I turn on the radio in the car and hear about another airplane crash, the stock market crash, and a pile up on the freeway. I come home at night and turn on the television to lull me to sleep. First I get a dose of people dying in an emergency room on *Grey's Anatomy*, then a man shot dead on rerun of *Cops*, then I catch a glimpse of a movie about a heinous murder. After that, there's the eleven o'clock news when I hear that a woman has been found dead in the Angeles National Forest, the apparent victim of yet another serial killer, and a woman has killed her own baby and told the police that the infant has been kidnapped. How can a person possibly be happy if all they see and hear is negative?

Every time you turn on the television, go to the movies, or pick up a newspaper or magazine you see everything that is wrong with our society. This is just junk food for your mind. Like your body, your mind needs to be fed good thoughts in order to create good feelings.

It's a dilemma. If you refuse to listen to what's going on, everyone will think you are an idiot and you don't care about what's going on in the world. If you keep abreast of what's going on, you are poisoning your mind. If you *choose* to be happy, I suggest that you adopt a program of feeding yourself this news in smaller doses. Limit yourself. You certainly don't need to spend money going to see violent movies after watching television, listening to the news or reading the paper. It's like washing down a box of chocolate donuts with some peanut brittle.

If you *choose* to be happy, focus on what is good in this world. You need to know what is happening in the world, but you don't need to saturate your mind with negative thoughts and injustices.

I remember taking a walk with Elizabeth in the park along Ocean Avenue in Santa Monica. The park was strewn with wall-to-wall homeless people and tattooed ex-cons. Elizabeth just kept on talking about something else as we stepped over bums sleeping all over the ground and ignored potential predators. To this day, I don't know if she noticed them or not. If she did, she refused to acknowledge anything negative about our walk.

Our media has made real life drama into live entertainment for us. It started with CNN's broadcast of The Gulf War. Millions of Americans were glued to their television sets and the concept of "reality television" was born.

Then there was the famous O. J. white Bronco chase in Los Angeles. Almost every day there is another police pursuit—some idiot wanting to be on the news. Then there was live coverage of "Shock and Awe" in Iraq and the media frenzy over the death of Anna Nicole Smith and her son. There was more interest in who was the "daddy" of Anna Nicole's baby than there was in Iran's nuclear threat.

We all seem to have developed an addictive craving for real life entertainment and "breaking news." Although it is good to keep informed about what is happening in the world, it is also necessary to your peace of mind and happiness to go on a "news fast." Did you ever notice that when you go on vacation and don't have the time or inclination to listen to the news, when you return home the world is still there as you left it, but you feel well-rested? Why not vow not to listen to the news on weekends? Or how about not listening to any news or magazine programs after 8:00 P.M.?

> ❧ *Protect yourself against what is wrong about this world.*
> *Focus on what is **right** with this world.* ❧

Trust Your Own Judgment

Recently I saw a segment on the one of the magazine programs in which they showed how a man used the Internet to research a cure for his young daughter's rare heart disease. Doctors told him that there was no cure, but on the Internet he was able to find a prescription for vitamins to treat this disease. He put his daughter on a regimen of these vitamins. Soon after, the doctors confirmed that his daughter's heart disease was cured. Had this man listened to his doctors and not taken matters into his own hands, I'm sure he would not have cured his daughter.

Create a Support System

Having a family is a basic human need that is almost as important as food, air and shelter. Teenagers join gangs in order to have a feeling of belonging to a family who cares about them. Other people join religious cults or various support groups in order to have a sense of belonging. If you don't have a family, you probably feel a deep sense of loss and aloneness that can make you very unhappy. If you have a family that doesn't live up to your expectations, your family's inner conflicts are probably making you unhappy.

Unfortunately, you cannot choose your family. But, luckily, you can choose your friends. One of the main secrets of happiness is having a sense of control over your life—and that includes the people with whom you choose to share your life. Take control of your life and your happiness by cultivating friends and co-workers who can fulfill your need for family.

Strive for Inner Peace

Inner peace is a sense of control over your feelings, your emotions and your environment. Everything is in order. It's like when you clean and straighten up your house and everything is sparkling and perfectly organized. That is what your body and mind feel like when you have inner peace.

Everyone has his or her own method of finding inner peace. Some pray. Some meditate. Others jog. Others lie on the couch and listen to music or watch television. There is no right or wrong method to achieve inner peace.

Take time to thank your Higher Spirit for what you do have, to ask for what you desire, and to ponder what is really important in your life. If you believe that some Higher Spirit or guardian angel is watching over you and guiding you, you will feel safer.

I believe that all human beings yearn for security and if you believe in a power more powerful than yourself, that you will feel more secure.

Listen to Your Body

Pain or discomfort is your body's way of telling you that something is wrong. Chronic headaches, stomach upsets, rashes, backaches, palpitations and anxiety attacks are your body's way of saying that it is out of balance with your mind and spirit.

If you do not learn to listen to your body, the gentle reminders will turn into thumps on the head. The headaches will turn into brain cancer, the stomach upsets will turn into bleeding ulcers, the rashes will turn into melanomas, the backaches will turn into tumors, the anxiety attacks will turn into nervous breakdowns, and the palpitations will turn into heart attacks.

Listen to your body as if it were your child crying for help. Give it the comfort and love it needs.

Is There a Secret of Happiness?

Some people believe that we keep on coming back over and over again until we finally learn the ultimate lesson of life. What I want to know is if there is anyone out there who has ever come back enough times to have actually learned the ultimate lesson of life? If so, please, tell us already, what is it?

I have no idea whether we come back to this life again and again or not. Since none of us really knows the truth about reincarnation, it is a good idea to create good karma just in case it is true. However, being a kind and caring person only because we think we are going to go to hell if we don't act that way is not really being kind and caring. Acting good and moral because you are afraid you are going to be reincarnated as a starving refugee or a monkey in a science lab is not the same as truly being good and moral.

Being a good person must come from your heart. You must *want* to be a good person. You must *want* to strive and learn to be a better person. Threat of punishment if you are not good does not change the core of your heart. In order to be happy, you must actually reprogram your inner thoughts so that they are always good and caring, but you must also forgive yourself for less than good and caring thoughts because you are only human.

Marianne Williamson, in *A Return to Love*, writes, "Love is what we were born with. Fear is what we have learned here. The spiritual journey is the relinquishment—or unlearning—of fear and the acceptance of love back into our hearts. Love is the essential existential fact. It is our ultimate reality and our purpose on earth. To be consciously aware of it, to experience love in ourselves and others, is the meaning of life."

Shirley MacLaine, in *Out on a Limb*, finds through her experiences with reincarnation that, ". . . negative exists because we make it so. We need to believe in a positive reality right here on earth because the believing will make it so . . . I don't worry about the past and I don't worry about the future, which the past created, and which is creating the future."

I personally believe that what you give to others in love and friendship, what you teach future generations, is the only part of you that lives on. You become the memory that lingers on in the hearts and minds of those whom you have touched. This is your soul. You may believe differently than this, and I respect whatever your beliefs are because nobody knows for sure.

Maxwell Maltz, author of the bestseller *Psycho-Cybernetics*, writes. "Happiness is simply a state of mind in which our thinking is pleasant a good share of the time . . . . Happiness is a mental habit and if it is not learned and practiced in the present, it is never experienced. It cannot be made contingent upon solving some external problem. When one life problem is solved another appears to take its place. Life is a series of problems. If you are to be happy at all, you must be happy—period—not happy because of something."

Maxwell Maltz suggests telling yourself the following eight statements every morning:

- I will be as cheerful as possible.
- I will try to feel and act a little friendlier toward other people.
- I am going to be a little less critical and a little more tolerant of other people, their faults, failings and mistakes. I will place the best possible interpretations upon their actions.
- I am going to act as if success was inevitable and I already am the sort of personality I want to be. I will practice "acting like" and "feeling like" this new personality.
- I will not let my own opinion color facts in a pessimistic or negative way.
- I will practice smiling at least three times during the day.
- Regardless of what happens, I will react as calmly and as intelligently as possible.
- I will ignore completely and close my mind to all those pessimistic and negative "facts" which I can do nothing to change.

Acting out these eight statements every day will remind you how to be happy and help fight your genetic unhappiness.

Werner Earhart, the ex-used-car salesman who started EST, told us that the secret of life is to not to row against the current of the river, but to *flow* with the current, which, of course, is still good advice.

Mihaly Csikszentmihalyi, professor of psychology at the University of Chicago, in his books, *Flow: the Psychology of Optimal Experience* and *The Evolving Self: a Psychology for the Third Millennium*, theorizes that "The more often people experience *flow*, the better they feel and function and the happier they are with their lives. You can turn dull activities into *flow* experiences by changing your approach. *Flow* is a process of discovering something new. The enjoyment that accompanies *flow* is the exhilaration that occurs when your body or mind is stretched to its limits in a voluntary effort to accomplish something difficult or worthwhile. The result is a strengthened sense of your abilities and yourself."

Csikszentmihalyi also writes, "When not focused on anything, our thoughts start to wander unpleasantly. It is like trying to listen to several conversations at once. We can't do it. This disorganization makes us anxious. Vague dread gnaws at us and we often fixate on our personal flaws."

Cynthia Hedricks, Ph.D., at the University of Southern California in Los Angeles, created the "Experience Sampling Method" in which participants carry pagers that go off randomly each day. Within minutes of being beeped, they answer questionnaires about what they are doing and what they are thinking and feeling. The results showed that most people experience *flow* anywhere from once in their lives to several times a day. It occurs when the activity is *autotelic*, which means that what you are doing is just for the sheer pleasure of doing it, not for any outside reward.

In an interview in *Shape* December 1996, Oprah Winfrey states, "Pure joy can only be felt when your mind is unattached to any other thought except what you're doing."

Stewart Emery started a group and wrote a book called *Actualizations* in which he said that to be self-actualized (happy) was to be real and to accept reality. True, too, but too simplistic for those of us complex souls who are genetically unhappy.

I suspect that none of us will ever be reincarnated enough times to get it right and learn the secret of happiness. This is because the secret of happiness is that there is no secret of happiness. Happiness is a state of being which comes and goes in accordance with the external events in our lives and how we perceive them internally.

No one is happy all the time. The pursuit of happiness is a perpetual process. Happiness is not an end result but rather an everyday process of enjoying what is good about your life while finding solutions to what is bad about your life.

Happiness is not just something you achieve and just lay back and enjoy. It is a *state of being* that you *choose* and that you work hard to maintain by remaining useful, curious and creative until the day you die.

Chapter 18

The Happiness Rules

Try to read through the "Happiness Rules" every morning before you even brush your teeth until they are embedded in your mind forever.

- Practice harmlessness of thoughts. Whenever you catch yourself making a nasty comment about someone, remember that it's *you* that you are harming.

- Practice harmlessness of words. Words are the weapons of your mind. They can pierce another person's heart.

- Practice harmlessness of actions. Your actions tell a story about who you are. If your actions are kind, you are kind. If your actions are mean, you are mean. You can't be mean and happy at the same time.

- Respect other people if you want to be respected.

- Don't be a jealous person. There is enough abundance and happiness in the world for everyone, including you.

- Learn from your mistakes. Mistakes are meant to teach you what you need to know in order to grow and be happy.

- Stop worrying. Take action instead.

- Accept that very few people can be trusted. But forgive them. It's not because they are bad; it's because they are just doing what they think they need to do in order to survive.

- Realize that everyone in the world is not out to get you nor to make your life miserable.

- Most people in this world really want to be kind and good, but there are still people who are mean and evil. Learn to trust the right people and stay away from the wrong people.

- Don't pass judgment on anyone. You don't know what she feels inside, what she has gone through, or what she must do in order to survive.

- If you don't like someone, don't make him into a friend, but have compassion. Try to understand the reasons why he does what he does or acts as he does.

- Don't complain. It accomplishes nothing but annoy other people.

- Turn arguments into discussions by refusing to blame, attack or criticize anyone. First, listen to what the other person is saying. Second, try to put yourself in her shoes and feel what she may be feeling. Third, even if you know you are right, be humble.

- Don't ever feel that you need to prove that you are right. Always admit that you *could be* wrong. Arguments usually happen when you hurt a person. His hurt turns into anger and then he lashes out at you. By making an effort to not hurt him, you can avoid most arguments.

- Be a good friend. You get back in life what you put out. If you are a good friend, you will attract good friends.

- Be assertive without being aggressive.

- Choose to see the best in everyone and to believe that most people are basically good and honest, but don't be a fool. Remember, if it sounds too good to be true, it *is* too good to be true.

- See your glass as half full, not half empty.

- Count your blessings the minute you get up every morning.

- Always thank your Higher Spirit for the gift of life that you have been given.

- Change the things that you can change and accept the things that you can't change.

- Like yourself and have a sense of humor about your own human flaws.

- Don't be self-absorbed.

- Don't obsess over your problems.

- Take care of your problems in the most efficient way you can and then move on.

- Give of yourself to others without expecting anything in return.

- Don't compare what you have to what others have and realize that life is not a contest of who has more.

- Make everyone you come in contact with feel happy.

- Make everyone you come in contact with feel important.

- Be compassionate, but know that you can't solve everyone else's problems.

- Have so many hobbies, interests and projects that you love that you are never bored.

- Be enthusiastic and passionate about life.

- Don't worry because it accomplishes nothing. Take action instead.

- Have a sense of humor. Laugh a lot and look for the humor in *every* situation.

- Don't focus on what is wrong with the world unless you are willing to do something to change it.

- Add something to society.

- Don't fear death.

- Learn to enjoy being alone without feeling lonely.

- Live in the present because the past is unchangeable and the future is unpredictable.

- Have nothing to hide. Keep no secrets.

- Forgive yourself for the mistakes you have made.

- Forgive others for their mistakes.

- Don't hold grudges. Grudges will eat away at you like a cancer.

- Don't harbor anger. It will poison your body.

- Don't hate anyone or anything. Hate is toxic.

- Have compassion for the unhappiness of others.

- Be aware and respectful of your environment at all times.

- Be smart enough to ignore the things that might sabotage your happiness.

- Strive to create a perfect balance in your life.

- Find a life work that you love.

- If you are not enjoying your work, either change your job or profession or change your attitude about it.

- Always make sure that you have an exciting reason to get up in the morning.

- Know when to plan your activities and when to be spontaneous.

- Have only one addiction—*happiness*.

- See every day and every problem as a new and exciting challenge.

- See the world as an exciting place to explore.

- Don't see the world as a scary place.

- Determine to overcome adversity.

- Be willing to take on a challenge.

- Take responsibility for your own needs.

- Takes responsibility for your own actions.

- Set realistic goals for yourself and others.

- Be willing to fail.

- Make an honest appraisal of your personal accomplishments.

- Come to terms with your strengths and weaknesses.

- Find successful and pleasurable ways to cope with stress.

- Enjoy simple pleasures.

- Don't be judgmental. It is not anyone's place to pass judgment on another human being. Other people are only acting out of their own experiences of life.

- Be generous. It will come back to you threefold.

- Feel a sense of connection with other people and with nature.

- Be confident and assertive.

- Be the master of your own destiny. Develop a strong sense of control over your life.

- Treat your body well.

- Never take your good health for granted.

- Stay healthy in order to enjoy high energy and stamina.

- Exercise regularly. It releases endorphins. Most previously depressed people who do cardiovascular exercise three or more times a week for more than 30 minutes report that they no longer feel depressed.

- Sleep restfully.

- Develop a strong network of family, friends and coworkers.

- Give and receive compliments graciously.

- Always speak well of yourself without bragging.

- Nicely let others know how you expect to be treated.

- Enjoy pleasure without guilt.

- Know that greed, hate and anger are the fatal flaws that will destroy your life.

- Always look and act approachable.

- Remember that what you wish upon others will come back to you—positive *and negative.*

- Know that hate is the venom of unhappiness.

- Know that love is the elixir of happiness.

- Focus on what you have, not on what is missing in your life.

- Always forgive.

- Learn from your mistakes.

- Stop sabotaging yourself by creating your own negative self-fulfilling prophecies.

- Find effective ways to handle stress. There is good stress that motivates us and keeps our energy up and there is bad stress that makes us sick. This is different for everyone. Don't judge the amount of stress that your body and mind can take by some-one else's stress tolerance. Be kind to yourself. If you know how much stress you can take, organize your life accordingly.

- Turn every negative into a positive.

- Develop a good sense of self-worth. If you believe you are worthy of being happy, you will be happy.

- Live in the here and now.

- Think of life as a wonderful game to be played.

- Don't allow your mind to tell you that you need certain things to be different in your life in order for you to be happy.

- Change your thought processes to think of desires as mere preferences. That way, when your desires are not met, you don't feel unhappy that you didn't get what you wanted.

- Accept that the world hasn't been making you unhappy, but that you've been making yourself unhappy.

- Accept that there is no such thing as total security because security comes from within.

- Stop going down the up escalator of life.

- Accept that if you are genetically unhappy, it's like being an alcoholic. You will always have a tendency to want to think and do things that will make you unhappy. Remember, you are a "recovering" unhappy person and must work harder than a genetically happy person does in order to be happy.

- Happiness is not based on what you have or what you want. When you finally get what you want, then you have to worry about holding on to it.

- Remember, as you think, you shall get. If you think small you will get small. So, think big.

The Happiness Workbook

Try to work on these every night before you go to sleep. That way your subconscious can work on *choosing* to be happy while you snooze peacefully.

- Write down all the people and situations in your life that are making you unhappy.

- Write down next to each item what steps you need to take in order to change or get rid of these people or situations.

- Take action. Free yourself of all the annoying people and situations in your life one by one.

- If that is not possible, write down a positive statement that will *change your attitude* about that person or situation and that will enable you to deal with the frustration and still be happy.

- Write down what is worrying you. Visualize the worst thing that will happen. If it's a predicament that you have control over, write down what you can do about it. If you have no control over the situation, give it over to your Higher Power. Put your worries to sleep and you will fall asleep more easily

- Think positive thoughts before you go to sleep. Never think about what you *do not* want. Always think about what you *do* want. Your subconscious mind attracts what it's thinking about. If you concentrate on wealth, you will receive wealth. You get from life exactly what you expect. As you are falling asleep, try to see your life as a pleasure that you have been blessed with and you will receive pleasure when you arise.

- Don't allow your fears a place in your subconscious. Negative thoughts attract negative results. If you allow your fears to occupy a space in your mind, your fears will attract the very thing you fear.

- Make positive affirmations like "I *can* lose weight," "I *will* get that job," or "I *am* healthy" right before you go to sleep. Your words will affect how you feel in the morning. If you want to be happy, use happy words.

Developing into a healthy, happy person from a genetically unhappy person is much like the process of a flower blossoming. As you open up your mind and your heart to others and practice acts of kindness and harmlessness of thoughts, you will naturally find the confidence to reach out to others, to take risks, to bond, to belong to groups and to find your place in society.

You will automatically develop the physical and mental energy to achieve your goals and dreams. Then you will develop the maturity and wisdom to accept your failures as a learning process and to keep on going despite adversity.

You will find inner peace when you have totally accepted yourself, your good points as well as your shortcomings. You will not have to prove anything to anyone, including yourself. You will be free to enjoy life at your own pace. You will love mankind. You will love yourself.

There is no shortage of happiness. It's yours for the taking. Free of charge. All you have to do is *choose* to be happy and reprogram your inner thoughts, attitudes and perceptions.

∽ *May happiness be yours forever!* ∽

Acknowledgements

I am deeply grateful to Nigel Yorwerth of PublishingCoaches.com for not only his work as my foreign rights agent, but as my advisor. I sincerely appreciate all the time and energy he spent helping me develop "Choose to Be Happy" to its fullest potential. He genuinely cared about my book as if it was his own and provided me with outstanding guidance and advice. Nigel, you are fabulous to work with and I am so sorry for driving you crazy, even on weekends. *You're terrific.*

I would also like to thank Josie Stewart, who did a fabulous job on the layout of my book and managed to piece together an Introduction that seemed to have a mind of its own. Her patience and personal interest in making my book *"special"* have endeared her to me and I will always trust Josie to lay out all my future "Choose To" books.

And, of course, my wonderful cousin Paula Shiller, who laboriously edited all my silly mistakes as she read it aloud to my 92-year-old Aunt Evelyn, who is legally blind. Paula, that was so sweet of you!

And to Tim Leonhart of BookMasters and Atlas Books, my printer and distributor, who patiently spent time with me explaining every aspect of the printing and publishing process. Tim, you never rushed me off the phone and always took the time to make sure I understood everything. You are wonderful to work with and I appreciate all the extra time and effort you put into making this project work.

And last but not least, thank you to James Bennett, who designed a cover that *wowed* me and made my book come to life. He captured the essence of what "Choose to Be Happy" is all about on his first try. Thank you James.

I somehow magically created an incredibly wonderful team, which is proof that if something is meant to be, it will happen easily. Each and every one of you is special and wonderful to work with and I hope to be working with you all for many years to come.

About the Author

Happiness Coach Rima Rudner is the published author of "The Complete Guide to Decorating Your Home: How to Become Your Own Interior Designer" as well as coauthor of "Who Moved My Birthday: The Baby Boomers Essential Guide to Anti-Aging," written with Dr. Brad Frank, MD, MPH, MBA, Dr. Sanjay Gupta, MD, and Richard Moon, RPh, FIACP.

Rima has written many screenplays, sitcoms, standup comedy routines, children's books and magazine articles. Her ghostwriting includes other self-help books on health and fitness, diet, anti-aging, psychology and relationships.

She has survived many life-threatening illnesses and accidents including a rare form of bladder cancer, viral spinal meningitis and a major ski accident. She always triumphs over adversity because she has a winning attitude and a sense of humor. Now she has decided to turn lemons into lemonade and shares how she has stayed happy despite so much adversity.

She lives in Pacific Palisades, California with her husband, Harvey, and her very mischievous Airedale, Charley.

Contact: rima@rimarudner.com

Website: ChooseToBeHappy.net or RimaRudner.com